A NEW OWNER'S
GUIDE TO
KEESHONDEN

JG-149

Overleaf: A Keeshond photographed by Isabelle Francais.

Opposite Page: A Keeshond owned by Barbara Carberry.

The Publisher wishes to acknowledge the following owners of the dogs in this book, including: Ellen and Peter Dowd, Kathi L. Fleischer, Carrie Gore, M. Grabowski, Evelyn and Leo Hamelin, Cathe and Maigan Harvey, Carole Henry, Debra Hodges, Kameo Kennels, Sherri Mitchell, Nadine Schramm, Cherrie Treber, Cynthia Turnbull, Janice Wanamaker, Paula Weiman, Donna Williams.

Photographers: Ashbey Photography, Peter and Ellen Dowd, Kathi L. Fleischer, Isabelle Francais, Gilbert Photography, C. Grabowski, M. Grabowski, Ludwig Photo, Perry Phillips Photography, Pets by Paulette, Karen Taylor.

The author acknowledges the contribution of Judy Iby for the following chapters in this book: Sport of Purebred Dogs, Health Care, Identification and Finding the Lost Dog, Traveling with Your Dog, and Behavior and Canine Communication.

Distributed in the UNITED STATES to the Pet Trade by T.F.H. Publications, Inc., 1 TFH Plaza, Neptune City, NJ 07753; on the Internet at www.tfh.com; in CANADA by Rolf C. Hagen Inc., 3225 Sartelon St., Montreal, Quebec H4R 1E8; Pet Trade by H & L Pet Supplies Inc., 27 Kingston Crescent, Kitchener, Ontario N2B 2T6; in ENGLAND by T.F.H. Publications, PO Box 74, Havant PO9 5TT; in AUSTRALIA AND THE SOUTH PACIFIC by T.F.H. (Australia), Pty. Ltd., Box 149, Brookvale 2100 N.S.W., Australia; in NEW ZEALAND by Brooklands Aquarium Ltd., 5 McGiven Drive, New Plymouth, RD1 New Zealand; in SOUTH AFRICA by Rolf C. Hagen S.A. (PTY.) LTD., P.O. Box 201199, Durban North 4016, South Africa; in JAPAN by T.F.H. Publications. Published by T.F.H. Publications, Inc.

MANUFACTURED IN THE
UNITED STATES OF AMERICA
BY T.F.H. PUBLICATIONS, INC.

A NEW OWNER'S GUIDE TO
KEESHONDEN

PETER AND ELLEN DOWD

Contents

2000 Edition

**The Keeshond's easy-going manner
enables him to get along with anyone.**

**The happy and energetic Keeshond is a
wonderful addition to any home.**

The Keeshond has a striking appearance and an alert, intelligent expression.

The Keeshond's playful nature and endearing personality attribute to the breed's growing popularity.

The sociable and fun-loving Keeshond makes an excellent companion for gentle children.

ORIGIN and History of the Keeshond

t seems a well-established fact that, aided by various steps and crosses, most breeds of dog have descended from *Canis lupus*, the wolf, particularly from the northern branch of the family known as the northern European gray wolf. How long it took for the wolf to move out of the forest and into man's cave dwellings is a point of conjecture. However, it seems obvious that observation of the wolf could easily have taught early man some effective hunting techniques that he, too, would be able to use advantageously. Also, many of the wolf's social habits might have seemed strikingly familiar to early man. The association grew from there.

The wolves that could assist in satisfying the unending human need for food were, of course, most highly prized. As the man-wolf relationship developed throughout the ages, it also

The Keeshond's distinctive coat and pretty features make him one of the most attractive and recognizable breeds today.

This Keeshond puppy takes time out to smell the flowers.

became increasingly obvious that certain descendants of these increasingly domesticated wolves could be used to assist man with survival pursuits in addition to hunting. Also highly valued were those wolves that were large enough to assist in hauling and the *wolf-cum-dog* that made some kind of warning sound when a marauding neighbor or beast of prey threatened.

Throughout the centuries, many descendants of the original wolf stock would acquire great anatomical changes with man's intervention and breeding manipulation. However, long before man began to change the size and shape of *Canis familiaris* (the domestic dog), there existed a branch of the family canid that, because of its close proximity to wolf ancestry, retained many of the wolf's physical characteristics.

Like their undomesticated ancestors, these dogs maintained the characteristics that protected them from the rugged environment of northern Europe. Weather-resistant coats protected them from rain and cold; a long coarse outercoat shed snow and rain and a dense undercoat insulated against sub-zero temperatures. These coats were especially abundant around the neck and chest, thereby offering double protection for the vital organs. Plumed tails could cover and protect the nose and mouth if the animal was forced to sleep in the snow. Small prick ears were not easily frostbitten or frozen. The muzzle had sufficient length to warm the frigid air before it reached the lungs. Leg length was sufficient to keep the chest and abdomen above the snow line. Tails were carried horizontally or up over the back rather than trailing behind in the snow.

Skeletal remains of these early wolf descendants have been found throughout Northern and central Europe, northern Asia, and the arctic regions of North America. They stand as the forerunners of what are commonly referred to as the Arctic or Nordic breeds.

The Keeshond's full coat is one of his most valuable assets. The weather-resistant coat, especially abundant around the neck and chest, helped protect against the harsh and rugged environment of northern Europe.

This group can be divided into four categories: hunting dogs (Norwegian Elkhound, Chow Chow, and Karelian Bear Dog), draft dogs (Alaskan Malamute, Siberian Husky), herding dogs (Samoyed, Swedish, and Finnish Lapphunds), and companions dogs (including most of the Spitz-type dogs—German Spitz, Japanese Spitz, Volpino Italiano, and Keeshond).

One specific branch of this family was known as *Canis familiaris palustris,* or more commonly and interchangeably known as both "the dog of the lake" and "peat bog dog." Skeletons of these Spitz-type dogs have been found in many places throughout northern Europe and are said to have existed in the late Stone Age. While the exact role that dogs had in the lives of the tribes they lived with cannot be fully identified, some breed historians suggest that they may have served as what we today have come to think of as guard dogs. These dogs offered protection, not in the sense of aggressiveness, but in sounding the alarm by barking when danger threatened. The alert nature, rapid vocal response, and protective devotion to home and hearth of the Spitz breeds of today certainly give credibility to this theory.

THE SPITZ BREEDS IN GERMANY

The Spitz breeds had already became popular in Germany in

The Keeshond was described by Count Eberhard zu Sayne, a baron who resided in Germany's Rhine Valley in the early 1500s, as a dog that was completely dedicated to protecting his master, home, and property.

the early 1500s. Count Eberhard zu Sayne, a baron who resided in Germany's Rhine Valley, is the first to have been known to refer to the dogs as "Spitz." The word "Spitz" is German for "sharp point." The Count described the dogs as having no real interest in hunting but total dedication to their master and to protecting home and property. Evidently, the Count had great influence in Germany in that from his first usage of the term "Spitz" in 1540, the word was not only included in the German vocabulary but also in dictionaries from that point on.

The Spitz dogs came in many sizes and colors, each being identified by a separate name within Germany. As these dogs migrated outside of Germany's borders to surrounding countries, yet other names were given to the dogs that were obviously of the same character and heritage. Sometimes the name referred to the particular duties assigned to the dogs. At other times, the breed or variety's name was the result of the town or province in which the breed was developed.

All these Spitz dogs, however, shared the same physical characteristics that had distinguished them for many centuries prior. For our purposes, it is more useful to look at how the Germans separated the varieties by size. This classification system was originally used in Germany and is used today by the Federacion Internationale Cynologique, which is the canine governing authority throughout Europe.

The Keeshond, known as the German Wolfspitz, is the largest of the five German Spitz breeds. It stands approximately 18 inches tall and is exclusively gray in color.

The Wolfspitz is the largest of the five German Spitz breeds. It stands approximately 18 or more inches tall at the shoulder. The only color allowed is gray.

The next largest in size is the Gross Spitz, sometimes called the Giant Spitz, which stands 16 inches and above at the shoulder. Colors are white, black, brown, and orange.

The Mittelspitze or Standard Spitz is ideally 11 to 14 inches and can be white, black, brown, wolf gray and orange. The Kleinspitz or Small Spitz is bred in white, black, brown, wolf gray, and orange and measures $8 \frac{1}{2}$ to 11 inches in height. The Zwergspitz (Dwarf Spitz) is white, black, brown, wolf gray, and orange and measures less than $8 \frac{1}{2}$ inches in height.

It is the German Wolfspitz, the largest Spitz, that we are primarily concerned with here. In France, this variety was known as Chiens Loup, in Italy as the Lupini, and in Holland as the Keeshond (pronounced caze-hawnd; plural—Keeshonden (caze-hawnd-en).

THE KEESHOND BREED GETS ITS NAME

In the late 1700s, the Keeshond was very well thought of in the Netherlands, and the breed flourished throughout the country. This was particularly the case in the southern provinces of Brabant and Limburg. It was there that the breed was taken on as mascot of the common Dutch Patriot Party, which opposed the supportors of the Prince of Orange as governor of the Netherlands.

The Keeshond breed acquired its name from Dutch Patriot leader Cornelius ("Kees") de Gyselear. It was Kees' own "hond" (dog) that became the emblem of the Dutch party.

The rebellious "Patriots" were led by Cornelius ("Kees") de Gyselear, and it was Kee's own "hond" (dog) that became the emblem of the Dutch party and from which the breed was to have derived its proper name.

Alas, it was the House of Orange that was to emerge victorious in the political struggle, and the Patriot's party slipped into general disregard along with their Keeshonden, which were then considered affiliates of the defeated. In fact, much of the breed was destroyed by owners who did not want to appear to be Patriot sympathizers. Only country-folk farmers and those who operated the barges that proliferated in the Netherlands retained any loyalty to the breed. For a full century, the gentle and devoted Keeshonden languished in obscurity, serving primarily as watchdogs and pest controllers on the river boats, farms, and barges.

However, Miss J. G. Van der Blom and later the Baroness van Hardenbroek would take the breed in hand and through their efforts revive interest in these dogs in the Netherlands. Miss Van der Blom showed her first Keeshond in 1891 in Amsterdam. The breed's beauty and success in the show ring attracted fanciers and led to the importation of more stock

The Keeshond's sweet nature and striking appearance have attributed to his growing popularity.

from Germany. The breed's admirers established the Nederlandse Keeshond Club in 1924.

It was at this point that the success of Baroness van Hardenbroek's breeding program created interest in these dogs both at home and throughout Europe and England. A staunch supporter of the breed, it was the Baroness who led the resistance to Germany's attempts to have the breed officially called the German Wolfspitz in the Netherlands. Her adamant dedication to the Keeshond name influenced the breed club that was established in England in 1925. The club initially named itself the Dutch Barge Dog Club but changed it to The Keeshond Club just a year later.

In England, Mrs. Winfield Digby and Mrs. Alice Gatacre spearheaded interest in the Keeshond, and England's fanciers developed the breed to such a high level that the quality dogs exported are considered to be the root stock of America's entire bloodlines, except for a few isolated exceptions.

THE KEESHOND IN AMERICA

The first litter of Keeshonden was born in America in 1929. The litter was bred by Carl Hinderer, who had immigrated from Stuttgart, Germany, to Baltimore, Maryland, in 1923 and brought breeding stock with him. Through his efforts, the breed was given official recognition by the American Kennel Club (AKC) as a member of the Non-Sporting Group in 1930. The first 17 of the breed to be registered were all Carl Hinderer's imports and their offspring. Unfortunately, almost the entire breeding program was wiped out by distemper a short time later.

The Keeshond is a delightful breed that has captured the attention of many dedicated purebred dog fanciers.

Hinderer's efforts were not entirely in vain, however; it is because of him that interest in the breed grew to the point that the Keeshond Club of America, as it was to be named later, was organized in 1935. The breed also got the attention of many knowledgeable and influential dog fanciers along the East Coast and in the Midwest portions of the United States. Mr. and Mrs. Irving Florsheim were among the earliest active breeders and their Keeshond, Dochfour Hans, became the breed's first American-bred champion.

Mrs. Richard Fort, who lived in England, brought a number of her Kees with her to America early on in the breed's development in this country. Among them was Ch. Herzog, who became the first of the breed anywhere in the world to obtain a Companion Dog obedience degree. And to prove he was not simply all brains and no beauty, Herzog also won Best of Breed at the first Keeshond specialty held in the United States.

Since those early days, the breed has continually captured the interest of dedicated purebred dog fanciers but never the attention of those who would exploit the breed for commercial purposes. Those who have taken up the breed's cause have set quality control and steady improvement as their goal. Seventeen dogs were registered in 1930. Since then, the annual total has risen modestly, such that in 1998 the number of Keeshonden registered in the US was 1,769, placing the breed 66th among the 146 breeds registered by the AKC, and 107 were registered in the UK.

CHARACTERISTICS of the Keeshond

I f you haven't fully decided whether or not to add a Keeshond puppy to your life, a visit to a home or kennel to see a litter of puppies is probably not the best idea in the world—you will not leave without one! Kees puppies are absolutely irresistible. On a scale of 1 to 10, with 10 being the most irresistible, the Keeshond puppy would probably score 12 or more! There is absolutely nothing quite as captivating as these little bundles of fluff.

For this very reason, the person anticipating owning a Kees should give serious thought to the final decision. All puppies are cuddly and cute—particularly Kees puppies with their mischievous little expressions. Nor is there anything more enticing than a litter of Keeshond puppies at play or nestled together sound asleep, piled one on top of the other. But in addition to being cute, Kees puppies are living, breathing, and very mischievous little creatures. Not only that, they are totally dependent upon their human owner for *all* of their needs once they leave their mother and littermates.

Buying a dog, especially a puppy, before you are absolutely sure that you want to make that commitment can be a serious mistake. The prospective dog owner must clearly understand the amount of time and work involved in pet ownership. Failure to understand the extent of commitment involved is one of the primary reasons that there are so many unwanted canines that end their lives in an animal shelter.

Before anyone contemplates the purchase of a dog, there are some very basic conditions that must be considered. One of the first important questions that must be answered is whether or not the person who will ultimately be responsible for the dog's care and well-being actually wants a dog.

All too often it is the mother of the household who must shoulder the responsibility of the family pet's day-to-day care. While the children in the family, perhaps even the father, may be wildly enthusiastic about having a dog, it must be remembered that they are away most of the day at school or work. It is often Mom who will be taking on the additional responsibility of primary caregiver for the family pet.

Somehow this seems to be the case even when Mom works outside the home. Perhaps it's because mothers intuitively know when care is needed and that care of those dependent upon you is not something to be delayed. The question that demands an answer, then, is does she, in fact, share the enthusiasm for what could easily become another responsibility on her unending list?

Pets are a wonderful method of teaching children responsibility, but it should be remembered that the enthusiasm that inspires children to promise anything in order to have a new puppy may quickly wane. Who will take care of the puppy once the novelty wears off? *Does that person want a dog?*

Puppies are a huge responsibility and require a great deal of your time and attention. Make sure that you have made the right decision before bringing home a Keeshond puppy.

Desire to own a dog aside, does the lifestyle of the family actually provide for responsible dog ownership? If everyone in the family is away from early morning to late at night, who will provide for all of a puppy's needs? Feeding, exercise, outdoor access, and the like cannot be provided if no one is home.

Another important factor to consider is whether or not the breed of dog is suitable for the person or the family with which it will be living. A fully grown Kees can handle the rough and tumble play of young children. A very young Kees puppy may not be a good idea for a household in which the children have had no experience in dealing with baby animals.

Then, too, there is the matter of grooming. A luxuriously coated dog is certainly beautiful to behold, but all that hair takes a great deal of care. An adult Keeshond in full coat takes about one hour to thoroughly brush, but when he is shedding, it can take longer. Regular bathing can be difficult for some owners. It can be tedious to thoroughly wash and rinse the

A purebred Keeshond puppy will most likely grow up to look and act like his parents. dense coat, and drying it without the proper equipment is almost impossible. If this procedure cannot be performed properly at home, we strongly recommend that it be done by a professional groomer every two months.

As great as claims are for Kees intelligence and trainability, remember that every new dog must be taught the household rules which he is to observe. Some dogs catch on more quickly than others, and puppies are just as inclined to forget or to disregard lessons as young human children.

CASE FOR THE PUREBRED DOG

Although all puppies are cute, not all dogs grow up to be particularly attractive adults. What is considered beauty by one person is not necessarily seen as attractive by another.

It is almost impossible to determine what a mixed-breed puppy will look like as an adult. Nor is it possible to determine if the mixed-breed puppy's temperament will be suitable for the person or family who wishes to own it. If the puppy grows up to be too big, too hairy, or too active for the owner, what then will happen to it?

Size and temperament can vary to a degree, even within purebred dogs. Still, selective breeding over many generations has produced dogs that can give the would-be owner reasonable assurance of what the purebred puppy will look like and how he will behave as an adult. Aesthetics completely aside, this predictability is more important than one might think.

Puppies love to explore the world around them; however, a puppy's curious nature could get him into trouble if he is not properly supervised.

Purebred puppies will grow up to look like their adult relatives and will behave pretty much like the rest of their family. Any dog, mixed breed or not, has the potential to be a loving companion. However, the predictability of a purebred dog offers reasonable assurance that it will not only suit the owner's lifestyle but the person's aesthetic demands as well.

Before you bring a Keeshond puppy into your household, visit breeders and spend as much time with both puppies and adults as you can. Be sure that the *adult* Kees is a dog that appeals to you a esthetically and in temperament.

CHARACTER

The Keeshond has many wonderful personality traits and some that might be difficult to cope with for the wrong owner or the owner who is not careful to keep some of these characteristics under control while the dog is still young. This is not to say that an older dog cannot be retrained, but it is a far less difficult job to teach a Kees what is and isn't wanted in puppyhood than it is to convince the adult Kees that he no longer wants to behave in some way.

The Kees was bred and developed as a watch dog, and therefore he is very alert and has an acute sense of hearing. The breed is quick to warn you about visitors or intruders (both real and imagined!). In fact, one Kees owner told us that his dog's hearing was so highly developed he heard things *before* they even happened. Pete's parents have a retired champion of ours that can hear a car turn into a driveway 300 feet long!

There are some breeds that will never utter more than a whimper other than on a rare occasion. A Kees is not one of those dogs. On the other hand, a responsible owner can teach his Kees that barking for no reason at all is not acceptable.

Because of their acute sense of hearing and alert nature, Keeshonden make excellent watchdogs. This little puppy will grow into his role.

With their high degree of intelligence, Keeshonden tend to get bored easily. It is not a breed that can be left on its own continuously or kept outdoors alone. They are "people dogs"— denied the opportunity to be with those they love, a Kees can demand attention by becoming a problem barker. One of the breed's finest qualities is its desire to bond with and please its master. Not being allowed to do so can make even the best bred Kees unhappy and hard to live with.

This need to be close is very strong in the Keeshond. In fact, he can be underfoot just when you have forgotten he is there. This could be dangerous for someone who is not agile! But this need is born out of love and there is never any doubt that your Kees loves you. His love is absolutely unconditional. Even if his owner may be unfair or inconsiderate, the Kees continues to love with unflagging intensity.

The Keeshond is basically a very happy breed. In fact, there are those who say the term "jump for joy" was coined just for this breed. You will find a Kees completely capable of jumping

The Keeshond is known for his good temperament and excitability. Here, the term "jump for joy" fits perfectly.

several feet straight up in the air from a complete standstill. This is all well and good but might be intimidating for those who don't know your Duke or Duchess is simply happy. It is best to teach your Kees puppy early on that jumping up on people is definitely not allowed.

Since the Keeshond has no hunting or prey instinct, the breed gets along well with most other animals. Properly introduced, a Kees is happy to coexist with other dogs, cats, birds, and just about the entire animal spectrum.

STANDARD for the Keeshond

The AKC standard for the Keeshond is well-written in a straightforward manner that can be read and understood by even the beginning fancier. It must be understood, however, that it is only after many years of experience and observation that a person is really able to understand all the nuances of the breed. Also, standards are different in each country and you should refer to the Kennel Club in your own country for details. Reading as much as possible about the breed helps a great deal, but nothing benefits the novice more than putting himself in the hands of a dedicated and experienced breeder.

General Appearance—The Keeshond (pronounced *kayz-hawnd*) is a natural, handsome dog of well-balanced, short-coupled body, attracting attention not only by his coloration, alert carriage, and intelligent expression, but also by his stand-off coat, his richly plumed tail well curled over his back, his foxlike expression, and his small pointed ears. His coat is very thick around the neck, fore part of the shoulders and chest, forming a lion-like ruff—more profuse in the male. His rump and hind legs, down to the hocks, are also thickly coated, forming the characteristic "trousers." His head, ears, and lower legs are covered with thick, short hair.

Size, Proportion, Substance—The Keeshond is a medium-sized, square-appearing, sturdy dog, neither coarse nor lightly made. The ideal height of fully matured dogs when measured from top of withers to the ground is 18 inches for the males and 17 inches for bitches—a one inch variance either way is acceptable. While correct size is very important, it should not outweigh that of type.

Head—*Expression*—Expression is largely dependent on the distinctive characteristic called "spectacles"—a combination of markings and shadings in the orbital area which must include a delicate, dark line slanting from the outer corner of each eye toward the lower corner of each ear coupled with expressive eyebrows. Markings (or shadings) on face and head must present a pleasing appearance, imparting to the dog an alert and intelligent expression. **Very Serious Fault**: Absence of dark lines which form the "spectacles."

Eyes—Eyes should be dark brown in color, of medium size, almond shaped, set obliquely and neither too wide apart nor too close together. Eye rims are black. **Faults**: Round and/or protruding eyes or eyes light of color.

Ears—Ears should be small, triangular in shape, mounted high on the head and carried erect. Size should be proportionate to the head—length approximating the distance from the outer corner of the eye to the nearest edge of the ear. **Fault**: Ears not carried erect when at attention.

Skull—The head should be well-proportioned to the body and wedge-shaped when viewed from above—not only the muzzle, but the whole head should give this impression when the ears are drawn back by covering the nape of the neck and the ears with one hand. Head in profile should exhibit a definite stop. **Faults**: Apple head or absence of stop.

Muzzle—Of medium length, neither coarse nor snipey, and well proportioned to the skull.

Mouth—The mouth should be neither overshot nor undershot. Lips should be black and closely meeting—not thick, coarse or sagging—and with no wrinkle at the corner of the mouth. **Faults**: Overshot, undershot or wry mouth.

The Keeshond is a medium-sized dog with a square, sturdy body.

According to the standard, a Keeshond should possess an alert and intelligent expression.

Teeth—The teeth should be white, sound and strong, meeting in a scissors bite. **Fault**: Misaligned teeth.

Neck, Topline, Body—The *neck* should be moderately long, well-shaped and well set on shoulders. The body should be compact with a short, straight back sloping slightly downward toward the hindquarters: well-ribbed, barrel well rounded, short in loin, belly moderately tucked up, deep and strong of chest.

Tail—The tail should be moderately long and well feathered, set on high and tightly curled over the back. It should lie flat and close to the body. The tail must form a part of the "silhouette" of the dog's body, rather than give the appearance of an appendage. **Fault:** Tail not lying close to the back.

Forequarters—Forelegs should be straight seen from any angle. Pasterns are strong with a slight slope. Legs must be of good bone in proportion to the overall dog. Shoulder to upper arm angulation is between slight to moderate.

Hindquarters—Angulation in rear should be between slight to moderate to complement the forequarters, creating balance and typical gait. Hindquarters are well muscled with hocks perpendicular to the ground.

The Keeshond's head should be covered with smooth, soft, short hair—velvet-like in texture on the ears.

Feet—The feet should be compact, well rounded, cat-like. Toes are nicely arched with black nails.

Coat—The body should be abundantly covered with long, straight, harsh hair standing well out from a thick, downy undercoat. Head, including muzzle, skull and ears, should be covered with smooth, soft, short hair—velvety in texture on the ears. The neck is covered with a mane—more profuse in the male—sweeping from under the jaw and covering the whole of the front part of the shoulders and chest, as well as the top part of the shoulders. The hair on the legs should be smooth and short, except for feathering on the front legs and "trousers" on the hind legs. Hind legs should be profusely feathered down to the hocks—not below. The hair on the tail should form a rich

plume. Coat must not part down the back. The Keeshond is to be shown in a natural state with trimming permissible only on feet, pasterns, hocks and—if desired—whiskers. TRIMMING OTHER THAN AS DESCRIBED TO BE SEVERELY PENALIZED. **Faults**: Silky, wavy, or curly coats. Part in coat down the back.

Color and Markings—A dramatically marked dog, the Keeshond is a mixture of gray, black and cream. This coloration may vary from light to dark. The hair of the outer coat is black tipped, the length of the black tips producing the characteristic shading of color. Puppies are often less intensely marked. The undercoat is very pale gray or cream, never tawny.

Head—The muzzle should be dark in color. "Spectacles" and shadings, as previously described, are characteristic of the breed and must be present to some degree. Ears should be very dark—almost black.

Ruff, Shoulders and "Trousers"—The color of the ruff and "trousers" is lighter than that of the body. The shoulder line markings of light gray must be well defined.

Tail—The plume of the tail is very light in color when curled on the back, and the tip of the tail should be black.

Legs and Feet—Legs and feet are cream.

Faults: Pronounced white markings. Black markings more than halfway down the foreleg, penciling excepted. White foot or feet.

Very Serious Faults: Entirely black or white or any solid color; any pronounced deviation from the color as described.

Gait—The distinctive gait of the Keeshond is unique to the breed. Dogs should move boldly and keep tails curled over the back. They should move cleanly and briskly; the movement should be straight and sharp with reach and drive between slight to moderate.

Temperament—Temperament is of primary importance. The Keeshond is neither timid nor aggressive but, instead, is outgoing and friendly with both people and other dogs. The Keeshond is a lively, intelligent, alert and affectionate companion.

As one of their most impressive features, the Keeshond's coat is a dramatic mixture of gray, black, and cream, which may vary from light to dark.

Approved November 14, 1989
Effective January 1, 1990

SELECTING the Right Keeshond for You

WHAT TO LOOK FOR IN A BREEDER

Once the prospective Keeshond owner satisfactorily answers all of the questions relating to responsible ownership, he or she will undoubtedly want to rush out and purchase a puppy immediately. Take care not to act in haste. It is extremely important for the buyer of any dog to do his homework. This is very important because it is not possible to ask a breeder the right questions if you know nothing about the breed. Read as much as you can. There are many breed-specific and general care books in addition to this one that are available at local libraries and bookstores.

Although Keeshond puppies are often too adorable to resist, it's important to take the time to research the breed before bringing one home.

The purchase of any dog is an important step because the well-cared-for dog will live with you for many years. In the case of a Keeshond, this could easily be 13 to 14 years. You will undoubtedly want the pet you live with for that length of time to be one you will enjoy.

It is extremely important that your Kees is purchased from a breeder who has earned a reputation over the years for consistently producing dogs that are mentally and physically sound. There are always those who are ready and willing to exploit a breed for financial gain, with no thought given to its health or welfare, or to the homes in which the dogs will be living.

The only way a breeder can earn a reputation for quality is through a well-thought-out breeding program in which rigid

A physically and mentally sound puppy is the result of good quality breeding and excellent care.

selectivity is imposed. Selective breeding is aimed at maintaining the virtues of a breed and eliminating genetic weaknesses. This process is time-consuming and costly. Therefore, responsible Kees breeders protect their investment by providing the utmost in prenatal care for their brood matrons and maximum care and nutrition for the resulting offspring. Once the puppies arrive, the knowledgeable breeder initiates a well-thought-out socialization process.

The socialization process is not one to be overlooked. It is what produces a mentally sound dog that will be able to live with people in harmony. Keeshonden need human contact right from the beginning. It is important that the breeder spend a lot of time with each puppy individually in order to establish the human-canine relationship.

The first question a prospective owner should ask a breeder is, "What is the number one characteristic you breed for?" Deal only with those breeders that answer, "Good temperament." Anything else would be the first step on the road to tragedy.

A knowledgeable breeder will provide his or her puppies with adequate human contact. Puppies that are socialized at an early age will achieve their full potential as companions.

The buyer should also ask what the breeder *does* with his or her Kees. This will give some insight to the characteristics that a breeder is selecting for. Even if a breeder is attempting to breed outstanding show dogs, the responsible Kees breeder puts compatibility far ahead of any other characteristic. It will also tell the buyer if a breeder actually lives with his own dogs as pets–always a good sign.

The best puppies are born and raised in close proximity to their human family. Puppies raised in this way are imprinted with the scents and sounds of humans. Kees puppies born in a barn or garage and given few opportunities to be with humans seldom achieve their full potential as companions.

The buyer should look for cleanliness in both the dogs and the areas in which the animals are kept. Cleanliness is the first clue that tells you how much the breeder cares about the dogs he or she owns.

The governing kennel clubs in the different countries of the world maintain lists of local breed clubs and breeders that can lead a prospective dog buyer to responsible breeders of quality stock. If you are not sure where to contact a respected breeder in your area, contact your local kennel club for recommendations. Kennel club information can be found later in the book.

There is every possibility that a reputable breeder resides in your area who will not only be able to provide the right Kees for you, but who will often have both the parents of the puppy on the premises as well. This gives you an

opportunity to see firsthand what kind of dogs are in the background of the puppy you are considering.

Good breeders are not only willing to have you see their dogs, but will also allow you to inspect the facility in which the dogs are raised. They will be able to discuss problems that exist in the breed with you and how they deal with these problems. Do not be surprised if a concerned breeder asks many questions about you and the environment in which your Kees will be raised. Good breeders are just as concerned with the quality of the homes to which their dogs are going as you, the buyer, are in obtaining a sound and healthy dog.

Do not think a good Kees puppy can only come from a large kennel. On the contrary; today many of the best breeders raise dogs in their homes as a hobby. It is important, however, that you not allow yourself to fall into the hands of an irresponsible "backyard breeder." Backyard breeders separate themselves from hobby breeders through their lack of responsibility in bringing their breeding stock to its full potential. A hobby breeder's dogs find their way into the show and obedience ring or participate in the many and varied pursuits in which the Keeshond excels. Quite simply, a backyard breeder is an individual who simply breeds dogs for profit.

If there are no local breeders in your area, you can locate legitimate and reliable breeders throughout the country on the Keeshond Club or national kennel club lists. These established breeders are accustomed to safely shipping puppies to different states, even different countries.

Always check the references of these breeders and do not hesitate to ask for documentation. The breeder will undoubtedly have as many questions for you as you will have for him or her. When you call a far-away breeder, call at a reasonable hour and expect to have a lengthy discussion. The amount of money you invest in a satisfying telephone conversation may save you huge veterinary costs and a great deal of unhappiness.

Health Concerns

All breeds of dog have genetic problems that must be paid attention to, and just because a male and female do not show evidence of any problems does not mean their pedigrees are free of something that might be entirely incapacitating. Again, rely on recommendations from national kennel clubs or local breed clubs when looking for a breeder.

Health problems in any breed can only be eliminated by thoughtful breeders willing to breed selectively and discuss these issues openly. It is important that you ask the breeder you are considering about the following health concerns:

Hip Dysplasia: This is a malformation of the hip joints. It usually occurs bilaterally, meaning in both hips. It can occur in varying degrees from the mildest form, which is undetectable other than by x-ray, to extremely serious and painful cases that require surgery.

Having your Keeshond checked by a veterinarian on a regular basis can help detect problems before they become serious.

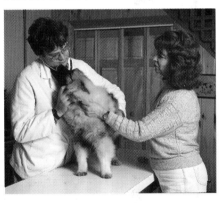

The normal hip can best be described as a ball-and-socket arrangement. The upper bone of the rear leg (femur) has a head that should fit neatly and firmly into the socket of the pelvis. A well-knit ball and socket allows the femur to rotate freely within the socket but is held firmly in place. When hip dysplasia exists, the socket is shallow, allowing the femur head to slip and slide to a greater or lesser degree. The more shallow the socket is, the more it impairs movement and causes pain.

Hypothyroidism: Hypothyroidism is a condition in which the thyroid gland malfunctions and its output is reduced. This happens when insufficient hormones are produced by an under active gland. It appears in a good many of the large-sized breeds. This condition can be diagnosed by a blood test.

Poor hair growth is often one of the first signs of this disease. Overall lethargy and weakness are typical symptoms, and though appetite may decrease, weight gain continues. Thyroid hormone administered daily can control the disease, but medication may be necessary for the dog's remaining life.

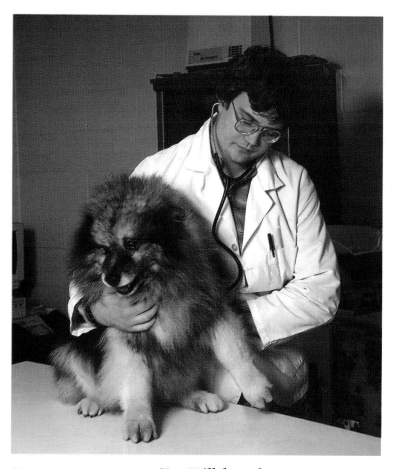

It's important that your Keeshond is comfortable and relaxed while being examined by the vet.

Von Willebrand's Disease (vWD): Though far from rampant in the breed, vWD should be mentioned. It is an abnormal condition of the blood-clotting system similar to, but in most cases not as severe as, hemophilia in human beings. It is seldom fatal, but can present a serious problem if surgery of any kind becomes necessary as uncontrolled bleeding can occur. Stress can bring on this condition, which is evidenced by mild bleeding from the nose and gums, and occasionally, bloody stools or urine. Research has revealed there is some evidence that the clinical severity of vWD decreases with age.

Patella Subluxation (Slipping Stifles): This is an abnormality of the stifle or knee joint leading to dislocation of the kneecap (patella). Normally, the kneecap is located in a groove at the lower end of the thighbone. It is held in this position by strong elastic ligaments. If the groove is insufficiently developed, the kneecap will leave its normal position and "slip" to one side or the other of the track in which it is normally held. Intermittent but persistent limp may occur or the dog may have difficulty straightening out the knee. Treatment may include surgery.

Breeders will do their best to match the right dog with the right home. For instance, a household with energetic children will need a playful and sociable puppy. These two pals share a bonding moment.

Epilepsy: This is a brief but overpowering disturbance of the nerve activity of the brain. The seizures are unprovoked, sudden, and convulsive and may be repeated at intervals. A number of medications can successfully treat the symptoms of epilepsy.

BUYER AND SELLER RESPONSIBILITY

It is impossible to sufficiently stress the importance of both the buyer and seller asking questions. This is not to say that the puppy you buy or his relatives will be afflicted with any of these conditions, but concerned breeders are well aware of their presence in the breed.

The dedicated breeder uses all of the answers you give him to match the right puppy with the right home. Households with boisterous children generally need a puppy that differs from one appropriate for a sedate, single adult. The time you invest in making the right selection ensures you of getting the right Kees for your lifestyle.

If questions are not asked, information is not received. We would be highly suspect of a person who is willing to sell you a Kees with "no questions asked."

Recognizing a Healthy Puppy

Most breeders in the US do not release their puppies until they have been given their "puppy shots." Normally, this occurs at about 7 to 9 weeks of age. At this stage, puppies will bond extremely well with their new owners and are entirely weaned.

Nursing puppies receive temporary immunization from their mother. Once weaned, however, a puppy is highly susceptible to many infectious diseases, which can be transmitted via the hands and clothing of people. Therefore, make sure your puppy is fully inoculated before he leaves his home environment and find out when any additional inoculations should be given.

Above all, the Kees puppy you buy should be a happy, bouncy extrovert. The worst thing you could possibly do is buy a shy, shrinking-violet puppy or one that appears sick and listless because you feel sorry for him. Doing this will undoubtedly lead to heartache and difficulty, to say nothing of the veterinary costs that you may incur in getting the puppy well.

If at all possible, take the puppy you are interested in away from his littermates and into another room or a different part of the kennel. Smells will remain the same, so the puppy should still feel secure and maintain his outgoing personality, but this will give you an opportunity to inspect the puppy more closely. A healthy little Kees puppy will be strong and sturdy to the touch, never bony or obese and bloated. The inside of the puppy's ears should be pink and clean. Dark discharge or a bad odor could indicate ear mites, a sure sign of poor maintenance. The healthy Kees puppy's breath smells sweet. His teeth are clean and white and there should never be any malformation of the mouth or jaw. The puppy's eyes should be clear and bright. Eyes that appear runny and irritated indicate serious problems.

Before you begin taking your Keeshond puppy outside of his home environment, make sure that he has had all of his inoculations.

There should be no sign of discharge from the nose, nor should it be crusted or runny. Coughing and diarrhea are danger signals, as are any eruptions on the skin. The coat should be soft and lustrous.

The healthy Kees puppy's front legs should be straight as little posts and the movement light and bouncy. The best way to describe a Kees puppy's movement is like that of a mechanical wind-up toy with legs that cover considerable ground. Of course, there is always a chubby, clumsy puppy or two in a litter. Do not mistake this for unsoundness, but if ever you have any doubts, discuss them with the breeder.

Remember, your pet will be living with you for a long time. Make sure the puppy reacts well to you. Run your fingers along the ground and see if he is willing to play. If the puppy has no interest in you, and the only thing he wants to do is get back to his littermates, definitely choose another puppy.

MALE OR FEMALE?

If you have decided on the sex of the puppy you want, do not let a breeder try to change your mind because that sex is not available. If you want a male, buy a male. This is one breed where there aren't many sex-related differences.

Actually, the biggest difference is in the coat. The mature male's coat is far more luxurious (and therefore requires more care for its upkeep). This can be compared to the growth pattern in lions—the hair is much longer and much thicker around the neck, shoulders, and chest of the male.

Females have their semiannual heat cycles once they have reached nine or ten months of age. During these heat cycles, which last approximately 21 days, the female must be confined to avoid soiling her surroundings with the bloody discharge that accompanies estrus. She must also be carefully watched to prevent males from gaining access to her or she could become pregnant.

While owners of other breeds find that training the male not to "lift his leg" and mark his territory indoors troublesome, most Kees males are not difficult to correct in this respect. Unless the dog has a highly developed herding instinct, Kees males seldom go wandering. They are far more interested in staying home to watch over their families.

It should be understood that most sexually related problems can be avoided by having the pet Keeshond "altered." Spaying the female and neutering the male saves the pet owner all the headaches of sexually related problems without changing the character of the breed. If there is any change at all in the altered Keeshond, it is in making the dog an even more amiable companion. Above all, altering your pet precludes the possibility of his adding to the serious pet overpopulation problems that exist worldwide.

Most breeders in the US who sell pet puppies have the buyer sign an agreement to have the puppy spayed or neutered before the registration certificate is released. This is a common practice that breeders employ to avoid having unscrupulous individuals breed pet-quality Keeshonden even though they have verbally agreed not to do so.

SELECTING A SHOW-PROSPECT PUPPY

It should be understood that the most any breeder can offer is an opinion on the "show potential" of a particular puppy. The most promising eight-week-old puppy can grow up to be a mediocre adult. A breeder has no control over this.

Male or female, a Keeshond is happiest when he is with his master, whether home in front of the TV or hiking a mountain trail. Dan and Debbie Dusylovitch with their favorite friend.

Any predictions breeders make about a puppy's future are based on their experience with past litters that have produced

winning show dogs. It is obvious that the more successful a breeder has been in producing winning Keeshonden over the years, the broader his or her base of comparison will be.

A puppy's potential as a show dog is determined by how closely he adheres to the demands of the standard of the breed. While most breeders concur that there is no such thing as "a sure thing" when it comes to predicting winners, they are also quick to agree that the older a puppy is, the better your chances are of making any predictions at all.

It makes little difference to the owner of a pet if the coat color of his Kees is not exactly as the standard describes or if an ear hangs down a bit. Neither would it make a difference if a male pup has only one testicle. These faults do not interfere with a Kees becoming a healthy, loving companion, although dogs that have one testicle have a high incidence of testicular cancer. However, these flaws would keep that Kees from a winning show career in the US.

While it certainly benefits the prospective buyer of a show-

A happy, outgoing attitude is an important thing to consider when searching for a show-prospect puppy.

If you are interested in showing your Keeshond, be sure that he adheres to the breed standard.

prospect puppy to be as familiar with the standard of the breed as possible, it is even more important for the buyer to put himself into the hands of a successful and respected breeder of winning Kees. The experienced breeder knows that there are certain age-related shortcomings in young Keeshonds that maturity will take care of and other faults that completely eliminate him from consideration as a show prospect. Also, breeders are always looking for the right homes in which to place their show-prospect puppies and will be particularly helpful in this respect when they know you plan to show one of their dogs.

The important thing to remember in choosing your first show prospect is that "cuteness" may not be consistent with quality. An extroverted puppy in the litter might decide he belongs to you. If you are simply looking for a pet, this is the puppy for you. However, if you are genuinely interested in showing your Kees, you must keep your head and, without disregarding good temperament, give serious consideration to what the standard says a show-type Kees must be.

The standard of the breed is presented in this book and its content is what, in the end, determines the show potential of a puppy. In selecting a show-quality puppy, all of the foregoing regarding soundness and health apply here as well. A point to remember, however, is that spaying and castration are not reversible procedures and once done will eliminate the possibility of ever breeding or showing your Kees in conformation shows. Altered dogs can, however, be shown in obedience and herding trials and many other competitive events.

There are a good number of additional points to be considered about the show dog as well. When selecting a show-quality puppy, we are looking for overall balance and that "look at me attitude" that is so important in the show ring.

Even in an eight-week-old puppy, we expect to see good movement and soundness, which are of paramount importance when a show dog is judged. The Kees must be sturdy but moderate in bone. Compact, balanced structure is typical of the breed, and concessions should not be made in this respect. It is also very important that a puppy be within the appropriate size range for his age.

A show dog is put under a lot more stress than a companion dog that spends his days at home. It is important that the show dog be able to hold up under the stress that will be created by frequent travel.

Puppy or Adult?

A young puppy is not your only option when contemplating the purchase of a Kees. In some cases, an adult dog or older puppy may be just the answer. It will certainly eliminate the trials and tribulations of housebreaking, chewing, and the myriad problems associated with a very young puppy. Inoculations become a once-a-year thing instead of frequent puppy shots. Very often the adult Kees will already be spayed or neutered.

Time should be allowed for an adjustment period, which can be longer for a mature dog than it might be for a very young puppy. A little extra attention can help a great deal in this respect.

Some adult Keeshonden may have become set in their ways and, while you may not have to contend with the problems of puppyhood, realize there may be the occasional adult that has developed habits not entirely suited to you or your lifestyle.

The Kees can and will get along well with all members of the animal family. However, if the adult dog has never spent time around other animals, you will have to introduce him gradually and carefully, making sure that the resident animal is not badgered or bullied by the more assertive Kees. In turn, the new Kees should not have to contend with aggressive behavior on the part of another dog or cat, even though he may have seniority.

A Keeshond that has never been around toddlers or very young children may be perplexed by these "miniature people." Introductions here should also take place gradually. Never allow children to chase after or grab at a Kees that is not accustomed to these little humans.

Arrange to bring an adult Kees into your home on a trial basis. This way neither you nor the dog will be obligated should either of you decide you are incompatible.

Keeshonden are very agreeable and usually have no problem interacting with animals, if you introduce them to the other pets in the household gradually and carefully.

IMPORTANT PAPERS

The purchase of any purebred dog in the US entitles you to three very important documents:

a health record containing an inoculation list, a copy of the dog's pedigree, and the registration certificate.

Health Record

Most Keeshond breeders have initiated the necessary inoculation series for their puppies by the time they are eight weeks of age. These inoculations protect the puppies against hepatitis, leptospirosis, distemper, and canine parvovirus. In most cases, rabies inoculations are not given until a puppy is four months of age or older.

There is a set series of inoculations developed to combat these infectious diseases, and it is extremely important that you obtain a record of the shots your puppy has been given and the dates upon which the shots were administered. In this way the veterinarian you choose will be able to continue with the appropriate inoculation series as needed.

Pedigree

The pedigree is your dog's "family tree." The breeder must supply you with a copy of a document authenticating your puppy's ancestry back to at least the third generation. All purebred dogs have a pedigree, which does not imply that a dog is of show quality. It is simply a chronological list of his ancestors.

Registration Certificate

The registration certificate is the canine world's birth certificate. This document is issued by a country's governing kennel club. When you transfer the ownership of your Kees from the breeder's name to your own name, the transaction is entered on this certificate. Once mailed to the kennel club, it is permanently recorded in their computerized files. Keep all of these documents in a safe place; you will need them when you visit your veterinarian or if you ever wish to breed or show your Kees.

It should be understood that it is common practice for some breeders to retain the registration certificate until the contractual spaying or neutering of the puppy is complied with.

DIET SHEET

Your Kees is the happy, healthy puppy he is because the

breeder has been carefully feeding and caring for him. Every breeder we know has his own particular way of doing this. Most will give the new owner a written record that details the amount and kind of food a puppy has been receiving. Follow these recommendations to the letter, at least for the first month or two after the puppy comes to live with you.

The diet sheet should indicate the number of times a day that your puppy is accustomed to being fed and the kind of vitamin supplementation he has been receiving if any. Following the prescribed procedure will reduce the chance of upset stomach and loose stools.

Your breeder should supply you with a diet sheet explaining your puppy's feeding schedule. Try to stick to the original diet for at least the first month after your puppy comes home.

Usually, a breeder's diet sheet projects the increases and changes in food that will be necessary as your puppy grows from week to week. If the sheet does not include this information, ask the breeder for suggestions regarding increases and the eventual changeover to adult food.

In the unlikely event that you are not supplied with a diet sheet by the breeder and are unable to get one, your veterinarian will be able to advise you in this respect. There are countless foods now being manufactured expressly to meet the nutritional needs of puppies and growing dogs. A trip down the pet aisle at your supermarket or pet supply store will prove just how many choices you have. Two important tips to remember: Read labels carefully for content, and deal with established, reliable manufacturers, because you are more likely to get what you pay for. Feeding and nutrition are dealt with in greater detail later in the book.

HEALTH GUARANTEE

Any reputable breeder is more than willing to supply a written agreement that the sale of your Kees is contingent upon several things. Although all are equally important, certainly the puppy must be able to pass a veterinarian's examination. Furthermore, the breeder should guarantee that the puppy will not develop any hereditary problems. Last but not least, the temperament of the puppy you purchase should be vouched for. There is a period of adjustment that all puppies go through when they first go to a new home, but it should be relatively short.

Ideally, you should be able to arrange an appointment with your chosen veterinarian right after you have picked up your puppy from the breeder and before you take the puppy home. If this is not possible, you should not delay this procedure any longer than 24 hours from the time you take your puppy home.

Although good temperament is inherited, you can help your Keeshond become a well-adjusted and happy dog by providing him with love, guidance, and companionship.

TEMPERAMENT AND SOCIALIZATION

Temperament is both hereditary and learned. Inherited good temperament can be ruined by poor treatment and lack of proper socialization. A Keeshond puppy that has inherited a bad temperament is a poor risk as a companion, show dog, or working dog and should never be bred from. Therefore, it is critical that you obtain a happy puppy from a breeder who is determined to produce good temperaments and has taken all of the necessary steps to provide the early socialization necessary.

It is important to remember that a Kees puppy may be as happy as a lark living at home with you and your family, but if the socialization begun by the breeder is not continued, that sunny disposition will not extend outside your front door. From the day the young Kees arrives at your home, you must be committed to accompanying him on an unending pilgrimage to meet and like all human beings and animals.

Puppy kindergarten and obedience classes are excellent choices for socialization. If you are fortunate enough to have a "puppy preschool" or dog training class nearby, attend with as much regularity as you possibly can. A young Kees that has been regularly exposed to other dogs from puppyhood will learn to adapt and accept other dogs and other breeds much more readily than one that seldom sees strange dogs.

Keeshonden are very high spirited when young and must be molded into their adolescence. If you have children well past the toddler stage in the household or living nearby, your socialization task will be assisted considerably.

Keeshonden raised with children seem to have a distinct advantage in socialization. The two seem to understand each other and in some way known only to the puppies and children themselves, give each other confidence to face the trying ordeal of growing up.

The children in your own household are not the only children your puppy should spend time with. It is a case of the more the merrier! Every child (and adult for that matter) that enters your household should be asked to pet your puppy.

According to the breed standard, the Keeshond's temperament should be outgoing and friendly with both people and other dogs.

Your puppy should go everywhere with you: the post office, the market, the shopping mall—wherever. Little Kees puppies create a stir wherever they go, and dog lovers will want to stop and pet the puppy. There is

In order to be a good show dog, your Keeshond will have to be comfortable with being handled by judges and performing in front of crowds.

nothing in the world better for the puppy. They are social dogs by nature. The breed standard calls for the Keeshond's temperament to be "outgoing and friendly with both people and other dogs."

If your Kees has a show career in his future, there are things in addition to being handled that will have to be taught. All show dogs must learn to have their mouths opened and inspected by the judge, who must be able to check the teeth. Males must be accustomed to having their testicles touched, as the dog show judge must determine that all male dogs are "complete," which means there are two normal-sized testicles in the scrotum. These inspections must begin in puppyhood and be performed on a regular and continuing basis.

THE ADOLESCENT KEESHOND

You will find it amazing how quickly that little ball of fur you first brought home begins to develop into a full-grown Keeshond. Some lines shoot up to full size very rapidly, others mature more slowly. Some Kees pass through adolescence quite gracefully, but most will grow out of their puppy fluff

Choose a good-quality dog food that is healthy and appropriate for your Keeshond's age and activity level. and become lanky and ungainly, growing in and out of proportion seemingly from one day to the next.

Food needs usually increase during this growth period. However, some Kees may seem as if they can never get enough to eat, while others experience a very finicky stage in their eating habits and seem to eat enough only to keep from starving. Think of Kees puppies as being as individualistic as children and act accordingly.

The amount of food you give your Kees should be adjusted to how much he will readily consume at each meal. If the entire meal is eaten quickly, add a small amount to the next feeding and continue to do so as the need increases. This method will ensure you of giving your puppy enough food, but you must also pay close attention to the dog's appearance and condition, as you do not want a Kees puppy to become overweight or obese.

At eight weeks of age, a Kees puppy is eating four meals a day. By the time the puppy is four months old, he can do well on two meals a day, fed morning and evening, with perhaps a snack in the middle of the day. If your puppy does not eat the food offered, he is either not hungry or not well. Your dog will eat when he is hungry. If you suspect your dog is not well, a trip to the veterinarian is in order.

After the dog is a year old, feed him once a day just before you eat your own dinner. In this way, a trip outdoors just before bedtime will usually ensure that the dog will spend an accident-free night.

Many dog owners feel their dogs need to be fed far more food than what they actually require. Over feeding is very harmful to dog's bodies. It puts stress on their kidneys and heart. It can also make them very lazy, which, in turn, will cause them to gain even more weight from lack of exercise.

During adolescence, your Keeshond may begin to test your authority. However, he needs your guidance and commitment to grow into a responsible and happy adult dog.

Feeding a diet too high in protein can be very harmful to the Keeshond in that it can lead to "hot spots" (eruptions in the skin). Remember, Kees are a long-haired breed and that coat keeps their bodies well insulated. Protein creates heat and too much can lead to skin problems.

This adolescent period is a particularly important and sometimes difficult one. Hormones are developing, and this can have an effect on the temperament of the dog. Boy puppies realize they are males and may test their ability to dominate. The girls tend to get silly. This is also the time your Kees must learn all of the household and social rules that he will live by for the rest of his life. Your patience and commitment during this difficult time will not only produce a respected canine good citizen, but will forge a bond between the two of you that will grow into a wonderful relationship.

CARING for Your Keeshond

The best way to make sure your Kees puppy is obtaining the right amount and the correct type of food for his age is to follow the diet sheet provided by the breeder from whom you obtained your puppy. Do your best not to change the puppy's diet and you will be less apt to run into digestive problems and diarrhea. Diarrhea is very serious in young puppies—they can dehydrate very rapidly causing severe problems and even death.

If it is necessary to change your Kees puppy's diet for any reason, it should be done gradually, over a period of several meals and a few days. Begin by adding a tablespoon or two of the new food, gradually increasing the amount until the meal consists entirely of the new product.

By the time your Kees is 10 to 12 months old, you can reduce feedings to once a day. This meal can be given either in the morning or evening. It is really a matter of choice on your part. There are two important things to remember: Feed the main meal at the same time every day and make sure what you feed is nutritionally complete.

The single meal can be supplemented by a morning or nighttime snack of hard dog biscuits made especially for smaller dogs. These biscuits not only become highly anticipated treats by your Kees, but are genuinely helpful in maintaining healthy gums and teeth.

Balanced Diets

In order for a canine diet to qualify as "complete and balanced" in the United States, it must meet standards set by the Subcommittee on Canine Nutrition of the National Research Council of the National Academy of Sciences. Most commercial foods manufactured for dogs meet these standards and prove this by listing the ingredients contained in the food on every package or can. The ingredients are listed in descending order, with the main ingredient listed first.

52

Fed with any regularity at all, refined sugars can cause your Kees to become obese and will definitely create tooth decay. Candy stores do not exist in the wild—canine teeth are not genetically disposed to handling sugars. Do not feed your Kees candy or sweets and avoid products that contain sugar to any high degree.

Fresh water and a properly prepared, balanced diet that contains essential nutrients in correct proportions are all that a healthy Keeshond needs to be offered. Dog foods come canned, dry, semi-moist, "scientifically fortified," and "all-natural." A visit to your local supermarket or pet store will reveal the vast array of foods available to select from.

It is important to remember that all dogs, whether they are Chihuahuas, Keeshonden, or Great Danes, are omnivores (meat- and plant-eating) animals. While the vegetable content of your Kees' diet should not be overlooked, a dog's

If you need to change your Keeshond's diet, do so gradually to avoid any digestive problems.

physiology and anatomy are based on carnivorous food acquisition. Protein and fat are absolutely essential to the well-being of your dog. In fact, it is wise to add a teaspoon or two of vegetable oil or bacon drippings to your dog's diet, particularly during the winter months in colder climates.

Read the list of ingredients on the dog food you buy. Animal protein should appear first on the label's list of ingredients. A base of quality kibble to which meat and even table scraps have been added can provide a nutritious meal for your Kees.

This having been said, it should be realized that carnivores in the wild eat the entire beast they capture and kill. The carnivore's kills consist almost entirely of herbivores (plant-eating) animals and invariably, the carnivore begins its meal with the contents of the herbivore's stomach. This provides the carbohydrates, minerals, and nutrients present in vegetables.

If you offer your Keeshond treats, make sure that they are nutritious and do not upset his regular diet.

Throughout centuries of domestication, our dogs were made entirely dependent upon us for their well-being. Therefore, we are responsible for duplicating the food balance that the wild dog finds in nature. The domesticated dog's diet must include protein, carbohydrates, fats, roughage, and small amounts of essential minerals and vitamins.

Finding commercially prepared diets that contain all of the necessary nutrients will not present a problem. It is important to understand, though, that these commercially prepared foods already contain all of the necessary nutrients your Kees needs. It is, therefore, unnecessary to add vitamin supplements to these diets in other than special circumstances prescribed by

If you are unsure of which vitamin supplements to give your Keeshond, consult your veterinarian. your veterinarian. Over-supplementation and forced growth are now looked upon by some breeders as major contributors to many of the skeletal abnormalities found in purebred dogs of the day.

Oversupplementation

A great deal of controversy exists today regarding the orthopedic problems, such as hip and patella (knee) dysplasia, that can afflict all breeds. Some experts claim that these problems are entirely hereditary conditions, but many others feel that they can be exacerbated by overuse of mineral and vitamin supplements for puppies.

In giving vitamin supplementation, *never* exceed the prescribed amount. Many Kees breeders insist that all recommended dosages be halved before including them in a dog's diet. Yet other breeders feel supplementation should not be given at all, believing a balanced diet that includes animal protein, plenty of milk products, some fat, and a small amount of bone meal to provide calcium is all that is necessary and beneficial.

Pregnant and lactating bitches may require supplementation of some kind, but here again it is not a case of "if a little is good, a lot would be a great deal better." Extreme caution is advised in this case, and a health care regimen would be best discussed with your veterinarian.

If the owner of a Keeshond normally eats healthy, nutritious food, there is no reason why his dog cannot be given table scraps. What could possibly be harmful in good nutritious food? Table scraps should be given only as part of the dog's meal and never from the table. A Kees that becomes accustomed to being hand fed from the table can quickly become a real pest at meal time. Also, dinner guests may find the pleading stare of your Kees less than appealing when dinner is being served.

Dogs do not care if food looks like a hot dog or a piece of cheese. Truly nutritious dog foods are seldom manufactured to look like food that appeals to humans. Dogs only care about how food smells and tastes. It is highly doubtful that you will be eating your dog's food, so do not waste your money on these "looks just like" products.

Along these lines, most of the moist or canned foods that have the look of "delicious red beef" look that way because they contain large amounts of red dye. They should not be fed to your Kees!

To test the dye content of either canned or dry foods, place a small amount of the food on an absorbent towel after it has been moistened or prepared for your dog. Allow the food to remain there for several hours. If the paper is stained, you can rest assured that your dog's coat will be stained as well. Furthermore, preservatives and dyes are no better for your Kees than they are for you.

Special Diets

There are now a number of commercially prepared diets for dogs with special dietary needs. The overweight, underweight, or geriatric dog can have his nutritional needs met, as can puppies and growing dogs. The calorie content of these foods is adjusted accordingly. With the correct amount of the right foods and the proper amount of exercise, your Kees should stay in top shape. Again, common sense must prevail. Too many calories will increase weight and cutting back on calories will reduce weight.

Occasionally, a young Kees going through the teething period or a female coming into season will go off their food. The concerned owner's first response is often to tempt the dog by hand-feeding special treats and foods that the problem eater seems to prefer. This practice only compounds the problem. Once a dog learns to play the waiting game, he will turn up his nose at anything other than his favorite food, knowing full well that what he *wants* to eat will eventually arrive.

No matter what the breed, all dogs need physical and mental stimulation. Playing with your Keeshond will help him get exercise and feel like part of the family.

Unlike humans, dogs have no suicidal tendencies. A healthy dog will not starve himself to death. He may not eat enough to keep himself in the shape we find ideal and attractive, but he will definitely eat enough to maintain himself. If your Kees is not eating properly and appears to be too thin, it is probably best to consult your veterinarian.

SPECIAL NEEDS OF THE KEESHOND

Exercise

Almost anything you can do, your Kees can do, within reason. Long morning walks, hikes over mountain trails, exploring tide pools along the beach—your Kees will enjoy and benefit from these activities as much as you will.

On the other hand, if your own exercise proclivities lie closer to a walk around the block than to a ten-mile marathon, your Kees can be just as satisfied. The Keeshond is not a breed

Design an exercise program that is appropriate for your Keeshond's age and activity level. Most dogs will be willing to do anything as long as their master is present.

that requires taking your energy level to the outer limits. Most Kees are very "busy" dogs and, in fact, if your Kees shares his life with young children or other dogs, he could easily be getting all of the exercise he needs to stay fit. The Kees is always ready for a romp or to invent some new game that entails plenty of aerobic activity.

Slow, steady exercise that keeps your companion's heart rate in the working area will do nothing but extend his life. If your Kees is doing all this with you at his side, you are increasing the chances that the two of you will enjoy each other's company for many more years to come.

Naturally, common sense must be used in determining the extent and intensity of the exercise you give your Keeshond. Remember, young puppies have short bursts of energy and then require long rest periods. No puppy of any breed should be forced to accompany you on extended runs. Serious injuries can result. Again, short exercise periods and long rest stops are appropriate for any Kees under 10 or 12 months of age.

Most adult Kees will willingly walk as far, perhaps farther, than their owners are inclined to go. Daily walks combined with some ball retrieving or game playing in the yard can keep the average Kees in fine fettle.

Hot Weather

Caution must be exercised in hot weather. Plan your walks for the first thing in the morning if at all possible. If you cannot arrange to do this, wait until the sun has set and the outdoor temperature has dropped to a comfortable degree.

Whereas the Keeshond adapts well to the cold weather, hot weather can present a big problem. It's best to leave your Keeshond inside a cool home on extremely hot days.

Dogs should never be left in a car in hot weather. Temperatures can soar in a matter of minutes, and your dog can die of heat exhaustion in less time than you would ever imagine. Rolling down the windows does not help and is dangerous because an overheated dog will panic and attempt to escape through the open window. A word to the wise—leave your Kees at home in a cool room on hot days.

Cold weather, even temperatures hovering around the zero mark, are no problem at all for the Keeshond. The only warm clothing required for your winter walks will be your own as long as the two of you keep moving. Do not, however, allow your Kees to remain wet if the two of you get caught in the rain. At the very least, you should towel dry him. Better still, use a blow dryer to make sure that your Kees is thoroughly dry and mat-free.

59

GROOMING Your Keeshond

The Keeshond is a natural breed that requires next to no clipping or trimming. Breeders are most adamant that Kees lovers not fall into grooming fads of any kind. Proper brushing is all the grooming that your Kees will ever need, unless he is going to a dog show.

PUPPY COAT

Undoubtedly, the breeder from whom you purchased your Kees puppy will have begun to accustom the puppy to grooming as soon as there was enough hair to brush. You must continue with grooming sessions or begin them at once if for some reason they have not been started. You and your Kees will spend many hours involved in this activity over a lifetime, so it is imperative that you both learn to cooperate in the endeavor and make it an easy and pleasant experience.

The first piece of equipment you will need to obtain is a grooming table, which can be built or purchased at your local pet emporium. Even a sturdy card table topped with a non-skid pad will suffice. Make sure the table is of a height at which you can work comfortably either sitting or standing. Adjustable-height grooming tables are available at most pet shops. Although you will buy it when your Kees puppy first arrives, anticipate your dog's full-grown size in making your purchase and select or build a table that will accommodate a full-grown Kees lying on his side.

You will also need to invest in two brushes, a steel comb, barber's scissors, and a pair of nail clippers. The two brushes that you will need are a wire slicker brush (also called a rake) and a pin brush, sometimes called a "Poodle brush." For the finish work, you will need a commercial coat conditioner and a spray bottle. Consider the fact that you will be using this equipment for many years, so buy the best of these items that you can afford.

Do not attempt to groom your Kees on the floor. A puppy will try to get away from you when he has decided enough is enough, and you will spend a good part of your time chasing him around the room. Sitting on the floor for long stretches of time is not the most comfortable position in the world for the average adult either.

The Kees puppy should be taught to lie on his side to be groomed. He will be kept in that position for most of the grooming process. The puppy will also have to be kept in the sitting and standing position, but the lying position takes the most time and is more difficult for him to learn. The Kees trained to lie quietly on his side will prove to be a true godsend when the dog is fully grown and has developed a mature coat.

Begin this training by picking the puppy up as you would a lamb with his side against your chest and your arms wrapped around the puppy's body. Lay the puppy down on the table and release your arms, but keep your chest pressed lightly down on the puppy's side. Speak reassuringly to the puppy, stroking his head and rump. (This is a good time to practice the stay command.) Do this a number of times before you attempt to do any grooming. Repeat the process until your puppy understands what he is supposed to do when you place him on the grooming table.

An adjustable grooming table is an excellent tool for grooming your Keeshond. "Sophia" patiently awaits her turn to get pampered.

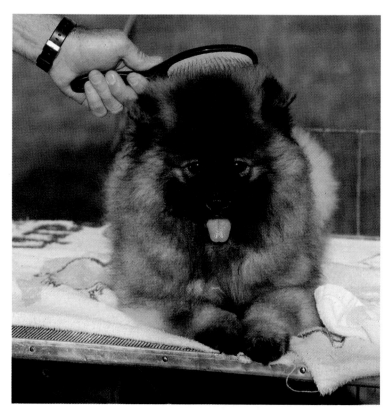

The Keeshond is a natural breed that requires minimal grooming. Proper brushing is all that your Keeshond needs to maintain a luxurious and attractive coat.

Using the slicker brush, begin what is called line brushing at the top of the shoulder at the base of the neck. Part the hair in a straight line from the front of the shoulder, straight on down to the bottom of the chest. Brush through the hair to the right and left of the part, lightly spraying the area with the coat conditioner as you go. Start at the skin and brush out to the very end of the hair. Do a small section at a time and continue on down the part. When you reach the bottom of the part, return to the top and make another part just to the right of the first line you brushed. *Part, brush, and spray.* You will repeat this process, working toward the rear, until you reach the puppy's tail.

It is preferable to do the legs on the same side you have been working on at this time. Be especially careful to attend to the hard-to-reach areas under the upper legs where they join the body. Mats occur in these areas very rapidly, especially when the Kees is shedding his puppy coat.

If you encounter a mat that does not brush out easily, use your fingers and the steel comb to separate the hairs as much as possible. Do not cut or pull out the matted hair. Apply baby powder or one of the especially prepared grooming powders directly to the mat and brush completely from the skin out.

If you can eliminate the tugging and tearing of your dog's coat in the detangling process, your dog will appreciate it, and his coat is less likely to be split or torn. Photo courtesy of Wahl, USA.

When you have finished the legs on one side, turn the puppy over and complete the entire process on the other side—*part, spray, brush*. As your Kees becomes accustomed to this process, you may find the puppy considers this naptime. You may have to lift your puppy into sitting position to arouse him from his slumber.

While the puppy is sitting, you can brush the hair of the chest and neck. Be particularly thorough in the area right behind the ears, as it is highly prone to matting. Use the line brushing method here as well. Next, stand the puppy up and brush the tail. Check the longer hair of the "pants" on the rear legs to make sure it is thoroughly brushed, especially around the area of the anus and genitalia. Needless to say, it is important to be extremely careful when brushing in these areas in that they are sensitive and easily injured.

Finishing Touches

When the line brushing process is completed, it is time for the finishing touches. Use your barber scissors to trim any long or shaggy hairs around your Kees's feet. You may trim off your Kees's whiskers if you wish. This is optional, however. Many Kees owners prefer to leave the whiskers on.

Brush the hair around the head, shoulders, and back forward. Do the same with the hair of the tail. Brush the chest hair downward and do the same with the hair on the sides of the dog.

Begin trimming your Keeshond's nails at an early age to help him get used to the procedure. It's important that he learns how to stay still or he could become injured.

Nail Trimming

This is a good time to accustom your Kees to having his nails trimmed and having his feet inspected. Always inspect your dog's feet for cracked pads. Check between the toes for splinters and thorns. Pay particular attention to any swollen or tender areas. In many sections of the country, there is a weed, sometimes called a "foxtail," which has a barbed hook-like affair that carries its seed. This hook easily finds its way into a Kees' foot or between his toes and very quickly works its way deep into the dog's flesh. This will very quickly cause soreness and infection. Foxtails are best removed by your veterinarian before serious problems result.

The nails of a Kees that spends most of his time indoors or on grass when outdoors can grow long very quickly. Do not allow the nails to become overgrown and then expect to cut them back easily. Each nail has a blood vessel running through the center called the quick. The quick grows close to the end of the nail and contains very sensitive nerve endings. If the nail is allowed to grow too long, it will be impossible to cut it back to a proper length without cutting into the quick. This causes the dog severe pain and can also result in a great deal of bleeding that can be very difficult to stop.

If your Kees is getting plenty of exercise on cement or rough hard pavement, the nails may stay sufficiently worn down. Otherwise, the nails can grow long very quickly. They must then be trimmed with canine nail clippers, an electric nail grinder (also called a dremel), or a coarse file made

expressly for that purpose. All three of these items can be purchased at major pet emporiums.

Many groomers prefer the electric nail grinder because it is so easy to control and helps avoid cutting into the quick. Kees have dark nails, which makes it practically impossible to see where the quick ends; so regardless of which nail trimming device is used, one must proceed with caution and remove only a small portion of the nail at time.

If you use the electric grinder, introduce it to your puppy at an early age. The instrument makes a whining sound not unlike a dentist's drill. The noise combined with the vibration of the sanding head on the nail itself can take some getting used to, but most dogs eventually accept it as one of life's trials.

Ch. Kameo's Nightwind Sonnet Moonpie and Whisper, owned by Kathi Fleischer, show off their perfectly groomed coats.

If the quick is nipped in the trimming process, there are a number of blood-clotting products available at pet shops that will almost immediately stem the flow of blood. It is wise to have one of these products on hand in case there is a nail trimming accident or the dog tears a nail on his own.

The adult Keeshond coat is different in texture and much longer and thicker than a puppy's coat. However, the brushing method is the same.

GROOMING THE ADULT KEESHOND

Hopefully, you and your Kees have spent the many months between puppyhood and full maturity learning to assist each other through the grooming process. The two of you have survived the shedding of the puppy coat and the arrival of entirely different adult hair. Not only is the Kees's adult hair of an entirely different texture, it is much longer and much thicker.

Undoubtedly, by this time you have realized that the pin brush with its longer bristles set in rubber is far more effective for line brushing the adult Kees than the slicker brush that you used through puppyhood. The method of brushing an adult coat is the same as that used when your Kees was a puppy. The obvious difference is that you have more dog and more hair.

While one might expect grooming an adult Kees to be a monumental task, this is not necessarily so. The two of you have been practicing the brushing routine for so long it has undoubtedly become second nature to both of you.

Additionally, the adult Kees's hair is actually much easier to cope with than the puppy coat. The ease of working with the Kees's adult coat, plus your own experience in the grooming routine, combine to make the task easier than what one might expect. Thoroughly grooming a fully mature Keeshond's coat will take an hour if done weekly. During the shedding period, which occurs twice a year, more time must be invested.

You will indeed have a difficult time ahead of you if the coat is neglected and becomes matted. Once the coat becomes "felted" with mats, you may have to resort to having a veterinarian or groomer shave the "matted to the skin" Kees. This should only be resorted to under extreme circumstances.

Some misguided owners feel that they are doing their dog a service by shaving his coat in summer, when exactly the opposite is true. The Kees's coat serves as insulation against both heat and cold, and the Kees's sensitive skin can become sunburned when the dog has been shaved.

BATHING

Regular coat care will keep a Keeshond's coat relatively clean; but like all dogs, the Kees has to be bathed in order to keep his coat odor-free. When you do bathe your Kees, never do so when the coat is matted. Wetting matted hair will only complicate the situation—the end result will provide you with much more work than if you had completed the mat removal process prior to bathing. On the rare occasions your Kees requires a wet bath, you will need to gather the necessary equipment ahead of time.

A rubber mat should be placed at the bottom of the tub to prevent your Kees from slipping and becoming frightened. A rubber spray hose is absolutely necessary to thoroughly wet the dense coat and to remove all shampoo residue.

A small cotton ball placed inside each ear will prevent water from running down into the dog's ear canal. A drop or two of mineral oil or a dab of petroleum jelly placed in each eye will preclude shampoo irritating the Kees's eyes.

It is best to use a shampoo designed especially for white dogs. The ph balance is adjusted to keep drying to a minimum and leaves the hair clean, shining, and lustrous.

To begin the bath, start behind the ears and work back. Use a washcloth to soap and rinse around the head and face. Once you have shampooed your Kees, you must rinse the coat thoroughly. When you feel quite certain that all shampoo residue has been removed, rinse once more. Shampoo residue in the coat is sure to dry the hair and could cause skin irritation.

As soon as you have completed the bath, use heavy towels to remove as much of the excess water as possible. Your Kees will assist you in the process by shaking a great deal of the water out of his coat on his own.

While your Kees's coat is still damp, it is best to blow dry it while brushing to prevent mats and tangles from forming. You can use either a human hair dryer or a special dog dryer to accomplish this task. Use the same brushing process you normally use.

If you admire the fluffy, well-groomed look of show dogs, like this Old English, you should consider using a hair dryer on your dog after his bath. Start using it when he's a pup so he will learn to enjoy the experience. Photo courtesy of Metropolitan Vacuum Cleaner Co., Inc.

HOUSEBREAKING and Training Your Keeshond

Any breed of dog can be trained. It does appear that some breeds are more difficult to get the desired response from than others. In many cases, however, this has more to do with the trainer and his training methods than the dog's inability to learn. With the proper approach, any dog that is not mentally deficient can be taught to be a good canine citizen. Many dog owners do not understand how a dog learns, nor do they realize that they can be breed-specific in their approach to training.

Young puppies have an amazing capacity to learn that is greater than most humans realize. It is important to remember, though, that these young puppies also forget quickly, unless they are reminded of what they have learned by continual reinforcement.

As puppies leave the nest, they began their search for two things: a pack leader and the rules set down by that leader. Because puppies, particularly Keeshond puppies, are cuddly and cute, some owners fail miserably in supplying these very basic needs to their dog. Instead, the owner immediately begins to respond to the demands of the puppy, and Kees puppies can quickly learn to be very demanding.

Puppies have an amazing capacity to learn. With the correct approach and guidance, you can train your Keeshond puppy to be an excellent canine citizen.

For example, a Kees puppy soon learns that he will be allowed into the house because he is barking or whining, not because he can only enter the house when he is *not* barking or whining. Instead of learning the only way he will be fed is to follow a set procedure (i.e., sitting or lying down on command), the Kees puppy learns that leaping about the kitchen and barking is what gets results.

If the young puppy cannot find his pack leader in an owner, he will assume the role of pack leader himself. The puppy learns to make his own rules when there are no rules imposed. And, unfortunately, the negligent owner continually reinforces the puppy's decisions by allowing him to govern the household.

The key to successful training lies in establishing the proper relationship between dog and owner. The owner or the owning family must be the pack leader and the individual or family must provide the rules by which the dog abides.

Once leadership is established, ease of training depends greatly on just how much a dog depends upon his master's approval. The entirely dependent dog lives to please his master and will do everything in his power to evoke the approval response from the person to whom he is devoted.

At the opposite end of the spectrum, we have the totally independent dog that is not remotely concerned with what his master thinks. Dependency varies from one breed to the next and, to a degree, within breeds as well. Kees are no exception to this rule. Fortunately for the owner, the average Kees falls somewhere near the middle of the dependency spectrum, and while certainly not a "pushover," the breed is highly trainable.

Establish the proper relationship with your Keeshond before you begin to train him. He needs to realize that you are in control and there are rules that he must follow.

Keeping your Keeshond puppy confined will lessen the chances of house-training accidents.

HOUSEBREAKING

The Crate Method

A major key to successfully training your Keeshond is *avoidance*, whether you are obedience training or housebreaking. It is much easier for your Kees to learn something if you do not first have to have him unlearn some bad habit. The crate training method of housebreaking is a highly successful method of preventing bad habits from starting.

First-time dog owners are inclined to initially see the crate or cage method of housebreaking as cruel, but those same people will return later and thank us profusely for having suggested it in the first place. They are also surprised to find that the puppy will eventually come to think of his crate as a place of private retreat—a den to which he will retreat for rest and privacy. The success of the crate method is based on the fact that puppies will not soil the area that they sleep in unless they are forced to do so.

Use of a crate or cage reduces housetraining time to an absolute minimum and keeps a puppy from being under constant stress by incessantly correcting him for making mistakes in the house. The anti-crate advocates consider it cruel to confine a puppy for any length of time, but find no problem in constantly harassing and punishing a puppy because he has wet on the carpet or relieved himself behind the sofa.

Crates and cages come in a wide variety of styles. The fiberglass shipping kennels used by many airlines are popular with many Kees owners, but residents of the warmer climates sometimes prefer the wire-type cage. Both are available at pet stores.

The cage or crate used for housebreaking should only be large enough allow the puppy to stand up, lie down, and stretch out comfortably. It is not necessary to dash out and buy a new cage every few weeks to accommodate the Kees' rapid spurts of growth. Simply cut a piece of plywood sized to partition off the excess space in the cage or crate and move it back as needed. Long before you have lost the need for the partition, your Kees will be housebroken.

Begin using the crate by feeding your Kees puppy his meals in it. Keep the door closed and latched while the puppy is eating. When the meal is finished, open the cage and *carry* the puppy outdoors to the spot where you want him to learn to eliminate. In the event that you do not have outdoor access or will be away from home for long periods of time, begin housebreaking by placing newspapers in some out of the way corner that is easily accessible to the puppy. If you consistently take your puppy to the same spot to relieve himself, you will reinforce the habit of going there for that purpose.

It is important that you do not let the puppy loose after eating. Young puppies will eliminate almost immediately after eating or drinking. They will also be ready to relieve themselves when they first wake up and after playing. If you keep a watchful eye on your puppy, you will quickly learn when this is about to take place. A puppy usually circles and sniffs the floor just before he relieves himself. Do not give your puppy an opportunity to learn that he can eliminate in the house! Your housetraining chores will be reduced considerably if you avoid this from happening in the first place.

If you are not able to watch your puppy every minute, he should be in his crate with the door securely latched. Each time you put your puppy in the crate, give him a small treat of some kind. Throw the treat to the back of the crate and encourage the puppy to walk in on his own. When he does so, praise the puppy and perhaps hand him another piece of the treat through the opening in the front of the crate.

Do not succumb to your puppy's complaints about being in the crate. He must learn to stay there and to do so without unnecessary complaining. A quick "no" command and a tap on the crate will usually get the puppy to understand that theatrics do not result in liberation. (Remember, as the pack leader, you make the rules, and the puppy wants to learn what they are!)

You can help your puppy feel more comfortable in his crate by putting some of his favorite toys, warm bedding, and food inside.

A Kees puppy that is 8 to 12 weeks of age will not be able to contain himself for long periods of time. Puppies that age must relieve themselves every few hours, except at night. Your schedule must be adjusted accordingly. Also, make sure that your puppy has relieved himself (both bowel and bladder) the last thing every night and do not dawdle when you wake up in the morning.

Your first priority in the morning is to get the puppy outdoors. Just how early this ritual will take place will depend much more on your puppy than on you. If your Kees is like most other puppies, there will be no doubt in your mind when he needs to be let out. You will also quickly learn to tell the difference between the this-is-an-emergency complaint and the "I just want out" grumbling. Do not test the young puppy's ability to contain himself. His vocal demands to be let out are confirmation that the housebreaking lesson is being learned.

When you find it necessary to be away from home all day, you will not be able to leave your puppy in a crate. On the other hand, do not make the mistake of allowing your puppy to roam the house or even a large room at will. Confine the puppy to a very small room or partitioned area and cover the floor with newspaper. Make this area large enough that the puppy will not have to relieve himself next to his bed, food, or water bowls. You will soon find that the puppy will be inclined to use one particular spot to perform his bowel and bladder functions. When you are home, you must take the puppy to this exact spot to eliminate at the appropriate time.

BASIC TRAINING

Your emotional state and the environment in which you train are just as important to your dog's training as the dog's state of mind at the time. Never begin training when you are irritated, distressed, or preoccupied. Nor should you begin basic training in a place that interferes with your dog's concentration. Once the commands are understood and learned, you can begin testing your dog in public places. At first, however, the two of you should work in a place where you can concentrate fully upon each other and the lesson at hand.

You must remain aware of a Kees's sensitivity level and his desire to please. Never resort to striking your Kees puppy. A very stern "No!" is usually more than sufficient and even in response to the most persistent unwanted behavior, striking the ground with a rolled-up newspaper is about as extreme as you will ever need to be.

The No Command

There is no doubt whatsoever that one of the most important commands your puppy will ever learn is the no command. It is critical that the puppy learns this command as soon as possible. One important piece of advice in using this and all other commands—*never give a command you are not prepared and able to enforce!* A good leader does not enforce rules arbitrarily. The only way a puppy learns to

Training your dog in a relaxing and open environment that is free of distractions will help him stay focused and motivated.

obey commands is to realize that once issued, commands must be complied with. Learning the no command should start on the first day of the puppy's arrival at your home.

Leash or Lead Training

Begin leash training by putting a soft, light collar on your puppy. After a few hours of occasional scratching at the unfamiliar object, your puppy will quickly forget it is even there.

It is not necessary for the puppy or adult Kees to wear his collar and identification tags within the confines of your home, and constant use will only serve to damage the dog's beautiful lion-like mane. However, no dog should ever leave home without a collar and a leash held securely in your hand. In some countries, dogs are required to be on lead at all times in public places.

Choose a lightweight collar for leash training. Your puppy may scratch at the unfamiliar object, but soon he will forget that he is even wearing one.

Begin getting your puppy accustomed to his collar by leaving it on for a few minutes at a time. Gradually extend the time you leave the collar on. Once this is accomplished, attach a lightweight leash to the collar while you are playing with the puppy. Do not try to guide the puppy at first. You are only trying to get him used to having something attached to the collar.

Have your puppy follow you as you move around by coaxing him with a treat of some kind. Let the puppy smell what you have in your hand and then move a few steps back, holding the treat in front of the puppy's nose. As soon as the puppy takes a few steps toward you, praise him enthusiastically and continue to do so as you move along.

Make the first few training sessions brief and fun for the puppy. Continue the lessons in your home or yard until the

Gradually increase the time that you leave a collar on your Keeshond. When he seems to be comfortable with it, attach a lightweight leash. puppy is completely unconcerned about the fact that he is on a leash. With a treat in one hand and a leash in the other, you can begin to use both to guide the puppy in the direction you wish to go.

Eventually, the two of you can venture out to the sidewalk in front of your house and then on to adventures everywhere! This is one lesson no puppy is too young to learn.

The Come Command

The next most important lesson for the Kees puppy to learn is to come when he is called. Therefore, it is very important that the puppy learns his name as soon as possible. Constant repetition is what does the trick in teaching a puppy his name. Use his name every time you talk to your puppy.

Learning to come on command could save your Kees's life when the two of you venture out into the world. "Come" is the command a dog must understand has to be obeyed without question; however, the dog should not associate that command with fear. Your Kees's response to his name and the word "come" should always be associated with a pleasant experience, such as great praise and petting or even a food treat.

Again, remember that it is much easier to avoid learning bad habits than it is to correct them once set. *Never* give the come command unless you are sure your puppy will come to you. A very young puppy is far more inclined to respond to learning the come command than an older dog. Young puppies are entirely dependent upon you. An older dog may lose some of that dependency and become preoccupied with his surroundings. So start your come-on-command training early.

Initially, use the command when the puppy is already on his way to you or give the command while walking or running away from the youngster. Clap your hands and sound very happy and excited about having the puppy join in on this "game."

The very young Kees puppy will normally want to stay as close to his owner as possible, especially in strange surroundings. When your Kees puppy sees you moving away, his natural inclination will be to get close to you. This is a perfect time to use the come command.

You may want to attach a long leash or rope to the puppy's collar to ensure the correct response. Do not chase or punish your puppy for not obeying the come command. Doing so in the initial stages of training will make the youngster associate the command with something to fear, and this will result in avoidance rather than the immediate positive response you desire. It is imperative that you praise your Kees puppy and give him a treat when he does come to you, even if he voluntarily delays responding for many minutes.

The Sit and Stay Commands

Just as important to your Kees' safety as the no command and learning to come when called are the sit and stay commands. Even a very young Kees can learn the sit command quickly, especially if it appears to be a game and a food treat is involved.

First, remember that the Kees in training should always be on a collar and leash for all of his lessons. A puppy is curious about everything that goes on around him and is not beyond getting up and walking away from his lesson when he has decided he needs to investigate something.

To begin, verbally give the sit command just before you reach down and exert pressure on your puppy's rear. Praise the puppy profusely when he does sit, even though it was you who exerted the effort. A food treat of some kind always seems to make the experience more enjoyable for the puppy.

Continue holding the dog's rear end down and repeat the sit command several times. If your puppy makes an attempt to get up, repeat the command yet again while exerting pressure on the rear end until the correct position is assumed. Make your puppy stay in this position a little bit longer with each succeeding lesson. Start with a few seconds and increase the time as lessons progress over the following weeks.

Teaching your Keeshond the come command gives him the freedom to play while keeping you in control of the situation.

If your puppy attempts to get up or to lie down, correct him by simply saying, "Sit!" in a firm voice.

This should be accompanied by returning the dog to the desired position. Only when *you* decide that your dog should get up should he be allowed to do so. Do not test the young Kees puppy's patience to the limit. Remember, you are dealing with a baby, and the attention span of any youngster is relatively limited. When you do decide that the dog can get up, call his name, say "OK," and make a big fuss over him. Praise and a food treat are in order every time your Kees responds correctly.

Once your puppy has mastered the sit lesson, you may start on the stay command. With your Kees puppy on leash and facing you, command him to "Sit," then take a step or two back. If your dog attempts to get up to follow, firmly say, "Sit, stay!" While you are saying this, raise your hand, palm toward the dog, and again command, "Stay!"

If your dog attempts to get up, you must correct him at once, returning him to the sit position and repeating, "Stay!" Once your Kees begins to understand what you want, you can gradually increase the distance you step back. With a long leash attached to your dog's collar, start with a few steps and gradually increase the distance to several yards. It is important that your dog learns that the sit/stay command must be obeyed no matter how far away you are. With advanced training, your Kees can be taught that the command is to be obeyed even when you leave the room or are entirely out of sight.

As your Kees becomes accustomed to responding to this lesson and is able to remain in the sit position for as long as you command, do not end the command by calling the dog to you. Walk back to your puppy and say, "OK." This will let your dog know that the command is over. When your Kees becomes entirely dependable in this lesson, you can then call the dog to you.

Have your puppy sit for things that he wants, such as a food treat or favorite toy. Always remember to praise him when he performs the correct behavior.

The sit/stay command can take considerable time and demands patience to get across to puppies. You must not forget that their attention span will be short. Keep the stay part of the lesson very short until your puppy is about 6 months old.

Because of its submissive position, the down command can be hard for puppies to master. However, it is very helpful in certain situations, as demonstrated here on the grooming table.

The Down Command

Do not try to teach your Kees puppy too many things at once. Wait until you have mastered one lesson quite well before moving on to something new.

When you feel quite confident that your puppy is comfortable with the sit and stay commands, you can start work on down. This is the single-word command for "lie down." Use the down command *only* when you want the dog to lie down. If you want your Kees to get off your sofa or to stop jumping up on people, use the *off* command. Do not interchange these two commands. Doing so will only confuse your dog so that evoking the right response will become next to impossible.

The down position is especially useful if you want your Kees to remain in one place for a long period of time. Most dogs are far more inclined to stay put if they are lying down rather than when they are sitting or standing.

Teaching this command to your Kees may take more time and patience than the previous lessons that the two of you have undertaken. It is believed by some animal behaviorists that assuming the down position somehow represents greater submissiveness.

Start the lesson with your Kees sitting in front of and facing you, hold a treat in your right hand and the excess part of the leash in your left hand. Hold the treat under the dog's nose and slowly bring your hand down to the ground. Your dog will follow the treat with his head and neck. As he does, give the command, "Down" and exert *light* pressure on the dog's shoulders with your left hand. If your dog resists the pressure on his shoulders, *do not continue pushing down*; doing so will only create more resistance. Reach down and slide the dog's feet toward you until he is lying down.

Retractable leashes provide dogs freedom while allowing the owner complete control. Leashes are available in a wide variety of lengths for all breeds of dog. Photo courtesy of Flexi-USA, Inc.

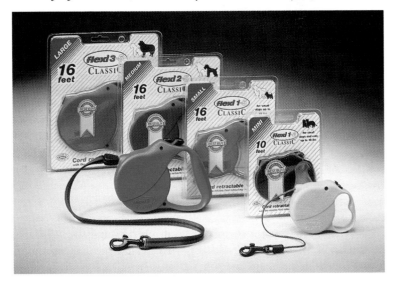

An alternative method of getting your Kees into the down position is to move around to the dog's right side and as you draw his attention downward with your right hand, slide your left hand under the dog's front legs and gently slide them forward. You will undoubtedly have to be on your knees next to the youngster in order to do this.

As your Kees's forelegs begin to slide out to his front, keep moving the treat along the ground until the dog's whole body is lying on the ground while you continually repeat, "Down." Once your dog has assumed the position you desire, give him the treat and a lot of praise. Continue assisting your puppy into the down position until he does so on his own. Be firm and patient.

Once your Keeshond is comfortable with his leash and collar, you can enjoy going outside for walks together.

The Heel Command

In learning to heel, your Kees will walk on your left side with his shoulder next to your leg, no matter which direction you might go or how quickly you turn. Teaching your Kees to heel is critical to off-leash control and will not only make your daily on-leash walks far more enjoyable, it will make your dog a far more tractable companion when the two of you are in crowded or confusing situations. We do not recommend ever allowing your Kees to be off leash when you are away from home, but it is important to know you can control your dog no matter what the circumstances are.

A lightweight, link-chain training collar is the best to use for the heeling lesson, and changing to this collar for the lesson indicates that what you are doing is "business" and not just a casual stroll. These link-chain collars provide quick pressure around the neck and a snapping sound, both of which get a dog's attention. Although they are sometimes called "choke collars," rest assured that when used properly, it will not choke the dog. The pet shop at which you purchase this training collar will be able to show you the proper way to put it on your dog.

As you train your Kees puppy to walk on leash, you should accustom the youngster to walking on your left side. The leash should cross your body from the dog's collar to your right hand. The excess portion of the leash will be folded into your right hand and your left hand on the leash will be used to make corrections with the leash.

If your Keeshond is having difficulty learning any of the commands, slow down and help him understand what he is supposed to do before progressing in the lesson.

A quick, short jerk on the leash with your left hand will keep your puppy from lunging side to side, pulling ahead, or lagging back. As you make a correction, give the heel command. Keep the leash loose when your dog maintains the proper position at your side. If your dog begins to drift away, give the leash a sharp jerk and guide the dog back to the correct position as you give the "heel" command. Do not pull on the leash with steady pressure—what is needed is a sharp but gentle jerking motion to get your dog's attention.

TRAINING CLASSES

There are few limits to what a patient, consistent Keeshond owner can teach his or her dog. Kees are highly trainable. Once lessons are mastered,you will find that most Kees will perform with the enthusiasm and gusto that make all your hard work well worthwhile.

For advanced obedience work beyond the basics, it is wise for the Kees owner to consider local professional assistance.

Professional trainers have had long-standing experience in avoiding the pitfalls of obedience training and can help you to avoid them as well.

This training assistance can be obtained in many ways. Classes are a particularly good way for your dog to learn how to obey commands amidst the distraction of all the interesting sights and smells of other dogs. There are free classes at many parks and recreation facilities, as well as formal and sometimes very expensive individual lessons with private trainers.

Keeshonden are a highly trainable breed and should not have any problems mastering the basic commands. This handsome Keeshond performs the sit.

There are also some obedience schools that will train your Kees for you. However, unless your schedule provides no time at all to train your dog, having someone else train him for you would be last on our list of recommendations. The rapport that develops between the owner who has trained his Kees and the dog himself is incomparable. The effort you expend to teach your dog to be a pleasant companion and good canine citizen pays off in years of enjoyable companionship.

VERSATILITY

There is no limit to the number of activities you and your Keeshond can enjoy together. The breed is highly successful in both conformation shows and obedience trials.

Canine Good Citizen certificates can be earned at conformation shows. An event called agility, which is actually an obstacle course for dogs, is not only fun for dog and owner, but many Kees owners find that their dogs are particularly well suited to this event.

Owners not inclined toward competitive events might find enjoyment in having their Kees's serve as therapy dogs. Dogs used in this area are trained to assist the sick, the elderly, and often the handicapped. Therapy dogs also make visits to hospitals and homes for the aged. It has been proven that these visits provide great therapeutic value to patients.

The well-trained Keeshond can provide a whole world of activities for the owner. You are limited only by the amount of time you wish to invest in this remarkable breed.

SPORT of Purebred Dogs

Welcome to the exciting and sometimes frustrating sport of dogs. No doubt you are trying to learn more about dogs or you wouldn't be deep into this book. This section covers the basics that may entice you, further your knowledge and help you to understand the dog world.

Dog showing has been a very popular sport for a long time and has been taken quite seriously by some. Others only enjoy it as a hobby.

The Kennel Club in England was formed in 1859, the American Kennel Club was established in 1884 and the Canadian Kennel Club was formed in 1888. The purpose of these clubs was to register purebred dogs and maintain their Stud Books. In the beginning, the concept of registering dogs was not readily accepted. More than 36 million dogs have been enrolled in the AKC Stud Book since its inception in 1888. Presently the kennel clubs not only register dogs but adopt and enforce rules and regulations governing dog shows, obedience trials and field trials. Over the years they have fostered and encouraged interest in the health and welfare of the purebred dog. They routinely donate funds to veterinary research for study on genetic disorders.

Successful showing requires a lot of dedication and patience. Training to compete in events should be an enjoyable experience for both dog and owner.

Below are the addresses of the kennel clubs in the United States, Great Britain and Canada.

The American Kennel Club
260 Madison Avenue
New York, NY 10016
(Their registry is located at: 5580
Centerview Drive, STE 200, Raleigh, NC
27606-3390)

The Kennel Club
1 Clarges Street
Piccadilly, London, WIY 8AB, England

The Canadian Kennel Club
100-89 Skyway Avenue
Etobicoke, Ontario M6S 4V7
Canada

In order to compete in shows, your Keeshond has to fit the breed standard. Here, Ch. O'Delyn Bet Your Boots, along with the author, shows off his winning looks.

Today there are numerous activities that are enjoyable for both the dog and the handler. Some of the activities include conformation showing, obedience competition, tracking, agility, the Canine Good Citizen Certificate, and a wide range of instinct tests that vary from breed to breed. Where you start depends upon your goals which early on may not be readily apparent.

PUPPY KINDERGARTEN

Every puppy will benefit from this class. PKT is the foundation for all future dog activities from conformation to "couch potatoes." Pet owners should make an effort to attend even if they

Puppy kindergarten provides your puppy with solid training skills, as well as the chance to interact with other puppies.

never expect to show their dog. The class is designed for puppies about three months of age with graduation at approximately five months of age. All the puppies will be in the same age group and, even though some may be a little unruly, there should not be any real problem. This class will teach the puppy some beginning obedience. As in all obedience classes the owner learns how to train his own dog. The PKT class gives the puppy the opportunity to interact with other puppies in the same age group and exposes him to strangers, which is very important. Some dogs grow up with behavior problems, one of them being fear of strangers. As you can see, there can be much to gain from this class.

There are some basic obedience exercises that every dog should learn. Some of these can be started with puppy kindergarten.

Recall

This quite possibly is the most important exercise you will ever teach. It should be a pleasant experience. The puppy may learn to do random recalls while being attached to a long line such as a clothes line. Later the exercise will start with the dog sitting and staying until called. The command is "Beau, come." Let your command be happy. You want your dog to come willingly and faithfully. The recall could save his life if he sneaks out the door. In practicing the recall, let him jump on you or touch you before you reach for him. If he is shy, then kneel down to his level. Reaching for the insecure dog could

frighten him, and he may not be willing to come again in the future. Lots of praise and a treat would be in order whenever you do a recall. Under no circumstances should you ever correct your dog when he has come to you. Later in formal obedience your dog will be required to sit in front of you after recalling and then go to heel position.

CONFORMATION

Conformation showing is our oldest dog show sport. This type of showing is based on the dog's appearance—that is his structure, movement and attitude. When considering this type of showing, you need to be aware of your breed's standard and be able to evaluate your dog compared to that standard. The breeder of your puppy or other experienced breeders would be good sources for such an evaluation. Puppies can go through lots of changes over a period of time. Many puppies start out as promising hopefuls and then after maturing may be disappointing as show candidates. Even so this should not deter them from being excellent pets.

Usually conformation training classes are offered by the local kennel or obedience clubs. These are excellent places for training puppies. The puppy should be able to walk on a lead before entering such a class. Proper ring procedure and technique for posing (stacking) the dog will be demonstrated as well as gaiting the dog. Usually certain patterns are used in the ring such as the triangle or the "L." Conformation class, like the PKT class, will give your youngster the opportunity to socialize with different breeds of dogs and humans too.

It takes some time to learn the routine of conformation showing. Usually one starts at the puppy matches that may be AKC Sanctioned or Fun Matches. These matches are generally for puppies from two or three months to a year old, and there may be classes for the adult over the age of 12 months. Similar to point shows, the classes are divided by sex and after completion of the classes in that breed or variety, the class winners compete for Best of Breed or Variety. The winner goes on to compete in the Group and the Group winners compete for Best in Match. No championship points are awarded for match wins.

A few matches can be great training for puppies even though there is no intention to go on showing. Matches enable the puppy to meet new people and be handled by a stranger—the judge. It is also a change of environment, which broadens the horizon for both dog and handler. Matches and other dog activities boost the confidence of the handler and especially the younger handlers.

Earning an AKC championship is built on a point system, which is different from Great Britain. To become an AKC Champion of Record the dog must earn 15 points. The number of points earned each time depends upon the number of dogs in competition. The number of points available at each show depends upon the breed, its sex and the location of the show. The United States is divided into ten AKC zones. Each zone has its own set of points. The purpose of the zones is to try to equalize the points available from breed to breed and area to area. The AKC adjusts the point scale annually.

Even if you don't plan to show your Keeshond, every puppy will benefit from basic training to make him a valued companion and member of the community.

The number of points that can be won at a show are between one and five. Three-, four- and five-point wins are considered majors. Not only does the dog need 15 points won under three different judges, but those points must include two majors under two different judges. Canada also works on a point system but majors are not required.

Dogs always show before bitches. The classes available to those seeking points are: Puppy (which may be divided into 6 to 9 months and 9 to 12 months); 12 to 18 months; Novice; Bred-by-Exhibitor; American-bred; and Open. The class winners of the same sex of each breed or variety compete against each other for Winners Dog and Winners Bitch. A

Reserve Winners Dog and Reserve Winners Bitch are also awarded but do not carry any points unless the Winners win is disallowed by AKC. The Winners Dog and Bitch compete with the specials (those dogs that have attained championship) for Best of Breed or Variety, Best of Winners and Best of Opposite Sex. It is possible to pick up an extra point or even a major if the points are higher for the defeated winner than those of Best of Winners. The latter would get the higher total from the defeated winner.

At an all-breed show, each Best of Breed or Variety winner will go on to his respective Group and then the Group winners will compete against each other for Best in Show. There are seven Groups: Sporting, Hounds, Working, Terriers, Toys, Non-Sporting and Herding. Obviously there are no Groups at speciality shows (those shows that have only one breed or a show such as the American Spaniel Club's Flushing Spaniel Show, which is for all flushing spaniel breeds).

Earning a championship in England is somewhat different since they do not have a point system. Challenge Certificates are awarded if the judge feels the dog is deserving regardless of the number of dogs in competition. A dog must earn three Challenge Certificates under three different judges, with at least one of these Certificates being won after the age of 12 months. Competition is very strong and entries may be higher than they are in the US. The Kennel Club's Challenge Certificates are only available at Championship Shows.

In England, The Kennel Club regulations require that certain dogs, Border Collies and Gundog breeds, qualify in a working capacity (i.e., obedience or field trials) before becoming a full Champion. If they do not qualify in the working aspect, then they are designated a Show Champion, which is equivalent to the AKC's Champion of Record. A Gundog may be granted the title of Field Trial Champion (FT Ch.) if it passes all the tests in the field but would also have to qualify in conformation before becoming a full Champion. A Border Collie that earns the title of Obedience Champion (Ob Ch.) must also qualify in the conformation ring before becoming a Champion.

Author Peter Dowd pictured with Ch. O'Delyn Lonestar.

The US doesn't have a designation full Champion but does award for Dual and Triple Champions. The Dual Champion must be a Champion of

WINNERS
LEHIGH VALLEY
KENNEL CLUB
1982
GILBERT PHOTO

Handlers should wear comfortable clothing that complements the dog and allows them to move about freely. Ch. Fearless Flashy Gal shows off her winning smile.

Record, and either Champion Tracker, Herding Champion, Obedience Trial Champion or Field Champion. Any dog that has been awarded the titles of Champion of Record, and any two of the following: Champion Tracker, Herding Champion, Obedience Trial Champion or Field Champion, may be designated as a Triple Champion.

The shows in England seem to put more emphasis on breeder judges than those in the US. There is much competition within the breeds. Therefore the quality of the individual breeds should be very good. In the United States we tend to have more "all around judges" (those that judge multiple breeds) and use the breeder judges at the specialty shows. Breeder judges are more familiar with their own breed since they are actively breeding that breed or did so at one time. Americans emphasize Group and Best in Show wins and promote them accordingly.

The shows in England can be very large and extend over several days, with the Groups being scheduled on different days. Though multi-day shows are not common in the US, there are cluster shows, where several different clubs will use the same show site over consecutive days.

Westminster Kennel Club is our most prestigious show although the entry is limited to 2500. In recent years, entry has been limited to Champions. This show is more formal than the majority of the shows with the judges wearing formal attire and the handlers fashionably dressed. In most instances the quality of the dogs is superb. After all, it is a show of Champions. It is a good show to study the AKC registered breeds and is by far the most exciting—especially since it is televised! WKC is one of the few shows in this country that is still benched. This means the dog must be in his benched area during the show hours except when he is being groomed, in the ring, or being exercised.

Ch. Flakkee Sweepstakes, the top-winning Keeshond of all time. During his show career, "Sweeper" won 46 all-breed Bests in Show and 109 Non-Sporting Group Firsts.

Typically, the handlers are very particular about their appearances. They are careful not to wear something that will detract from their dog but will perhaps enhance it. American ring procedure is quite formal compared to that of other countries. There is a certain etiquette expected between the judge and exhibitor and among the other exhibitors. Of course it is not always the case but the judge is supposed to be polite, not engaging in small talk or acknowledging how well he knows the handler. There is a more informal and relaxed atmosphere at the shows in other countries. For instance, the dress code is more casual. I can see where this might be more fun for the exhibitor and especially for the novice. The US is very handler-oriented in many of the breeds. It is true, in most instances, that the experienced professional handler can present the dog better and will have a feel for what a judge likes.

In England, Crufts is The Kennel Club's own show and is most assuredly the largest dog show in the world. They've been known to have an entry of nearly 20,000, and the show lasts four days. Entry is only gained by qualifying through winning in specified classes at another Championship Show. Westminster is strictly conformation, but Crufts exhibitors and spectators enjoy not only conformation but obedience, agility and a multitude of exhibitions as well. Obedience was admitted in 1957 and agility in 1983.

If you are handling your own dog, please give some consideration to your apparel. For sure the dress code at matches is more informal than the point shows. However, you should wear something a little more appropriate than beach attire or ragged jeans and bare feet. If you check out the handlers and see what is presently fashionable, you'll catch on. Men usually dress with a shirt and tie and a nice sports coat. Whether you are male or female, you will want to wear comfortable clothes and shoes. You need to be able to run with your dog and you certainly don't want to take a chance of falling and hurting yourself. Heaven forbid, if nothing else, you'll upset your dog. Women usually wear a dress or two-piece outfit, preferably with pockets to carry bait, comb, brush, etc. In this case men are the lucky ones with all their pockets. Ladies, think about where your dress will be if you need to kneel on the floor and also think about running. Does it allow freedom to do so?

You need to take along dog; crate; ex pen (if you use one); extra newspaper; water pail and water; all required grooming equipment, including hair dryer and extension cord; table; chair for you; bait for dog and lunch for you and friends; and, last but not least, clean up materials, such as plastic bags, paper towels, and perhaps a bath towel and some shampoo— just in case. Don't forget your entry confirmation and directions to the show.

If you are showing in obedience, then you will want to wear pants. Many of our top obedience handlers wear pants that are color-coordinated with their dogs. The philosophy is that imperfections in the black dog will be less obvious next to your black pants.

Whether you are showing in conformation, Junior Showmanship or obedience, you need to watch the clock and be sure you are not late. It is customary to pick up your conformation armband a few minutes before the start of the class. They will not wait for you and if you are on the show grounds and not in the ring, you will upset everyone. It's a little more complicated picking up your obedience armband if you show later in the class. If you have not picked up your armband and they get to your number, you may not be allowed to show. It's best to pick up your armband early, but then you may show earlier than expected if other handlers don't pick up.

Customarily all conflicts should be discussed with the judge prior to the start of the class.

A family affair—all winners at Berks County Kennel Club show. Ch. O'Delyn Bet Your Boots winning Best of Breed and Ch. O'Delyn Best Bet Yet winning Best of Winners.

Junior Showmanship

The Junior Showmanship Class is a wonderful way to

build self confidence even if there are no aspirations of staying with the dog-show game later in life. Frequently, Junior Showmanship becomes the background of those who become successful exhibitors/handlers in the future. In some instances it is taken very seriously, and success is measured in terms of wins. The Junior Handler is judged solely on his ability and skill in presenting his dog. The dog's conformation is not to be considered by the judge. Even so the condition and grooming of the dog may be a reflection upon the handler.

Usually the matches and point shows include different classes. The Junior Handler's dog may be entered in a breed or obedience class and even shown by another person in that class. Junior Showmanship classes are usually divided by age and perhaps sex. The age is determined by the handler's age on the day of the show. The classes are:

Novice Junior for those at least ten and under 14 years of age who at time of entry closing have not won three first places in a Novice Class at a licensed or member show.

Novice Senior for those at least 14 and under 18 years of age who at the time of entry closing have not won three first places in a Novice Class at a licensed or member show.

Open Junior for those at least ten and under 14 years of age who at the time of entry closing have won at least three first places in a Novice Junior Showmanship Class at a licensed or member show with competition present.

Open Senior for those at least 14 and under 18 years of age who at time of entry closing have won at least three first places in a Novice Junior Showmanship Class at a licensed or member show with competition present.

Junior Handlers must include their AKC Junior Handler number on each show entry. This needs to be obtained from the AKC.

CANINE GOOD CITIZEN

The AKC sponsors a program to encourage dog owners to train their dogs. Local clubs perform the pass/fail tests, and dogs who pass are awarded a Canine Good Citizen Certificate. Proof of vaccination is required at the time of participation. The test includes:

A dog's condition, behavior, and appearance in the ring are usually a reflection upon the handler.

1. Accepting a friendly stranger.
2. Sitting politely for petting.
3. Appearance and grooming.
4. Walking on a loose leash.
5. Walking through a crowd.
6. Sit and down on command/staying in place.
7. Come when called.
8. Reaction to another dog.
9. Reactions to distractions.
10. Supervised separation.

If more effort was made by pet owners to accomplish these exercises, fewer dogs would be cast off to the humane shelter.

OBEDIENCE

Obedience is necessary, without a doubt, but it can also become a wonderful hobby or even an obsession. Obedience classes and competition can provide wonderful companionship, not only with your dog but with your classmates or fellow competitors. It is always gratifying to discuss your dog's problems with others who have had similar experiences. The AKC acknowledged Obedience around 1936, and it has changed tremendously even though many of the exercises are basically the same. Today, obedience competition is just that—very competitive. Even so, it is possible for every obedience exhibitor to come home a winner (by earning qualifying scores) even though he/she may not earn a placement in the class.

To become a Canine Good Citizen, your Keeshond must be able to perform a number of different behaviors, such as sitting on command and remaining in place.

Most of the obedience titles are awarded after earning three qualifying scores (legs) in the appropriate class under three different judges. These

Training for competition takes a lot of dedication and perseverance; however, the efforts are well worth the results. classes offer a perfect score of 200, which is extremely rare. Each of the class exercises has its own point value. A leg is earned after receiving a score of at least 170 and at least 50 percent of the points available in each exercise. The titles are:

Companion Dog—CD

This is called the Novice Class and the exercises are:

1. Heel on leash and figure 8	40 points
2. Stand for examination	30 points
3. Heel free	40 points
4. Recall	30 points
5. Long sit—one minute	30 points
6. Long down—three minutes	30 points
Maximum total score	200 points

Companion Dog Excellent–CDX
This is the Open Class and the exercises are:

1. Heel off leash and figure 8	40 points
2. Drop on recall	30 points
3. Retrieve on flat	20 points
4. Retrieve over high jump	30 points
5. Broad jump	20 points
6. Long sit–three minutes (out of sight)	30 points
7. Long down–five minutes (out of sight)	30 points
Maximum total score	200 points

Utility Dog–UD
The Utility Class exercises are:

1. Signal Exercise	40 points
2. Scent discrimination-Article 1	30 points
3. Scent discrimination-Article 2	30 points
4. Directed retrieve	30 points
5. Moving stand and examination	30 points
6. Directed jumping	40 points
Maximum total score	200 points

After achieving the UD title, you may feel inclined to go after the UDX and/or OTCh. The UDX (Utility Dog Excellent) title went into effect in January 1994. It is not easily attained. The title requires qualifying simultaneously ten times

To receive the Utility Dog (UD) title, your Keeshond must complete scent discrimination exercises.

in Open B and Utility B but not necessarily at consecutive shows.

The OTCh (Obedience Trial Champion) is awarded after the dog has earned his UD and then goes on to earn 100 championship points, a first place in Utility, a first place in Open and another first place in either class. The placements must be won under three different judges at all-breed obedience trials. The points are determined by the number of dogs competing in the Open B and Utility B classes. The OTCh title precedes the dog's name.

Competition can be quite stressful for both dog and owner. Fun Matches are more lenient and allow more room to learn ring procedure.

Obedience matches (AKC Sanctioned, Fun, and Show and Go) are usually available. Usually they are sponsored by the local obedience clubs. When preparing an obedience dog for a title, you will find matches very helpful. Fun Matches and Show and Go Matches are more lenient in allowing you to make corrections in the ring. This type of training is usually very necessary for the Open and Utility Classes. AKC Sanctioned Obedience Matches do not allow corrections in the ring since they must abide by the AKC Obedience Regulations. If you are interested in showing in obedience, then you should contact the AKC for a copy of the Obedience Regulations.

TRACKING

Tracking is officially classified obedience. There are three tracking titles available: Tracking Dog (TD), Tracking Dog Excellent (TDX), Variable Surface Tracking (VST). If all three tracking titles are obtained, then the dog officially becomes a CT (Champion Tracker). The CT will go in front of the dog's name.

A TD may be earned anytime and does not have to follow the other obedience titles. There are many exhibitors that prefer tracking to obedience, and there are others who do both.

Tracking Dog–TD

A dog must be certified by an AKC tracking judge that he is ready to perform in an AKC test. The AKC can provide the names of tracking judges in your area that you can contact for certification. Depending on where you live, you may have to travel a distance if there is no local tracking judge. The certification track will be equivalent to a regular AKC track. A regulation track must be 440 to 500 yards long with at least two right-angle turns out in the open. The track will be aged 30 minutes to two hours. The handler has two starting flags at the beginning of the track to indicate the direction started. The dog works on a harness and 40-foot lead and must work at least 20 feet in front of the handler. An article (either a dark glove or wallet) will be dropped at the end of the track, and the dog must indicate it but not necessarily retrieve it.

Tracking can be very rewarding for your Keeshond because it gives him a chance to use his natural ability to smell.

People always ask what the dog tracks. Initially, the beginner on the short-aged track tracks the tracklayer. Eventually the dog learns to track the disturbed vegetation and learns to differentiate between tracks. Getting started with tracking requires reading the AKC regulations and a good book on tracking plus finding other tracking enthusiasts. Work on the buddy system. That is—lay tracks for each other so you can practice blind tracks. It is possible to train on your own, but if you are a beginner, it is a lot more entertaining to track with a buddy. It's rewarding seeing the dog use his natural ability.

Tracking Dog Excellent–TDX

The TDX track is 800 to 1000 yards long and is aged three to five hours. There will be five to seven turns. An article is left at the starting flag, and three other articles must be indicated on the track. There is only one flag at the start, so it is a blind start. Approximately one and a half hours after the track is laid, two tracklayers will cross over the track at two different places

to test the dog's ability to stay with the original track. There will be at least two obstacles on the track such as a change of cover, fences, creeks, ditches, etc. The dog must have a TD before entering a TDX. There is no certification required for a TDX.

Variable Surface Tracking—VST

This test came into effect September 1995. The dog must have a TD earned at least six months prior to entering this test. The track is 600 to 800 yards long and shall have a minimum of three different surfaces. Vegetation shall be included along with two areas devoid of vegetation such as concrete, asphalt, gravel, sand, hard pan or mulch. The areas devoid of vegetation shall comprise at least one-third to one-half of the track. The track is aged three to five hours. There will be four to eight

To receive a Tracking Dog Excellent (TDX) title, a dog must be able to stay on the original track and handle at least two obstacles.

Agility competitions give your Keeshond the chance to demonstrate his athletic ability. "Sugarplum," owned by Nadine Schramm, flies through the tire with ease.

turns and four numbered articles including one leather, one plastic, one metal and one fabric dropped on the track. There is one starting flag. The handler will work at least 10 feet from the dog.

AGILITY

Agility was first introduced by John Varley in England at the Crufts Dog Show, February 1978, but Peter Meanwell, competitor and judge, actually developed the idea. It was officially recognized in the early '80s. Agility is extremely popular in England and Canada and growing in popularity in the US. The AKC acknowledged agility in August 1994. Dogs must be at least 12 months of age to be entered. It is a fascinating sport that the dog, handler and spectators enjoy to the utmost. Agility is a spectator sport! The dog performs off lead. The handler either runs with his dog or positions himself on the course and directs his dog with verbal and hand signals over a timed course over or through a variety of obstacles including a time out or pause. One of the main drawbacks to agility is finding a place to train. The obstacles take up a lot of space and it is very time consuming to put up and take down courses.

The titles earned at AKC agility trials are Novice Agility Dog (NAD), Open Agility Dog (OAD), Agility Dog Excellent (ADX), and Master Agility Excellent (MAX). In order to acquire an agility title, a dog must earn a qualifying score in its respective class on three separate occasions under two different judges. The MAX will be awarded after earning ten qualifying scores in the Agility Excellent Class.

Performance Tests

During the last decade the American Kennel Club has promoted performance tests–those events that test the different breeds' natural abilities. This type of event encourages a handler to devote even more time to his dog and retain the natural instincts of his breed heritage. It is an important part of the wonderful world of dogs.

General Information

Obedience, tracking and agility allow the purebred dog with an Indefinite Listing Privilege (ILP) number or a limited registration to be exhibited and earn titles. Application must be made to the AKC for an ILP number.

The American Kennel Club publishes a monthly *Events* magazine that is part of the *Gazette*, their official journal for the sport of purebred dogs. The *Events* section lists upcoming shows and the secretary or superintendent for them. The majority of the conformation shows in the US are overseen by licensed superintendents. Generally the entry closing date is approximately two-and-a-half weeks before the actual show.

Point shows are fairly expensive, while the match shows cost about one third of the point show entry fee. Match shows usually take entries the day of the show but some are pre-entry. The best way to find match show information is through your local kennel club. Upon asking, the AKC can provide you with a list of superintendents, and you can write and ask to be put on their mailing lists.

Obedience trial and tracking test information is available through the AKC. Frequently these events are not superintended, but put on by the host club. Therefore you would make the entry with the event's secretary.

As you have read, there are numerous activities you can share with your dog. Regardless what you do, it does take teamwork. Your dog can only benefit from your attention and training. We hope this chapter has enlightened you and hope, if nothing else, you will attend a show here and there. Perhaps you will start with a puppy kindergarten class, and who knows where it may lead!

A perfect shot of "Allie," owned by Cherrie Treber, as she glides over the bar jump.

HEALTH CARE

Veterinary medicine has become far more sophisticated than what was available to our ancestors. This can be attributed to the increase in household pets and consequently the demand for better care for them. Also human medicine has become far more complex. Today diagnostic testing in veterinary medicine parallels human diagnostics. Because of better technology we can expect our pets to live healthier lives thereby increasing their life spans.

THE FIRST CHECKUP

You will want to take your new puppy/dog in for his first checkup within 48 to 72 hours after acquiring him. Many breeders strongly recommend this checkup and so do the humane shelters. A puppy/dog can appear healthy but he may have a serious problem that is not apparent to the layman. Most pets have some type of a minor flaw that may never cause a real problem.

Unfortunately if he/she should have a serious problem, you will want to consider the consequences of keeping the pet and the attachments that will be formed, which may be broken prematurely. Keep in mind there are many healthy dogs looking for good homes.

This first checkup is a good time to establish yourself with the veterinarian and learn the office policy regarding their hours and how they handle emergencies. Usually the breeder or another conscientious pet owner is a good reference for locating a capable veterinarian. You should be aware that not all veterinarians give the same quality of service. Please do not make your selection on the least expensive clinic, as they may be short changing your pet. There is the possibility that eventually it will cost you more due to improper diagnosis, treatment, etc. If you are selecting a new veterinarian, feel free to ask for a tour of the clinic. You should inquire about making an appointment for a tour since all clinics are working clinics, and therefore may not be available all day for sightseers. You may worry less if you see where your pet will be spending the day if he ever needs to be hospitalized.

The Physical Exam

Your veterinarian will check your pet's overall condition, which includes listening to the heart; checking the respiration; feeling the abdomen, muscles and joints; checking the mouth, which includes the gum color and signs of gum disease along with plaque buildup; checking the ears for signs of an infection or ear mites; examining the eyes; and, last but not least, checking the condition of the skin and coat.

He should ask you questions regarding your pet's eating and elimination habits and invite you to relay your questions. It is a good idea to prepare a list so as not to forget anything. He should discuss the proper diet and the quantity to be fed. If this should

Take your Keeshond for regular checkups to prevent problems and maintain good health.

differ from your breeder's recommendation, then you should convey to him the breeder's choice and see if he

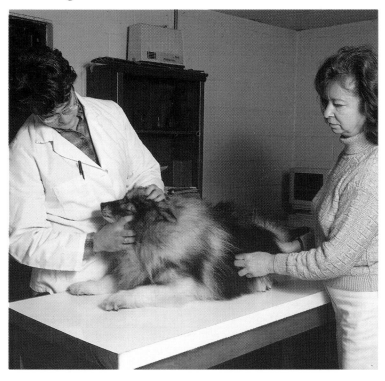

approves. If he recommends changing the diet, then this should be done over a few days so as not to cause a gastrointestinal upset. It is customary to take in a fresh stool sample (just a small amount) for a test for intestinal parasites. It must be fresh, preferably within 12 hours, since the eggs hatch quickly and after hatching will not be observed under the microscope. If your pet isn't obliging then, usually the technician can take one in the clinic.

It's important that you take your Keeshond's vaccination schedule with you on your first visit to the vet.

IMMUNIZATIONS

It is important that you take your puppy/dog's vaccination record with you on your first visit. In case of a

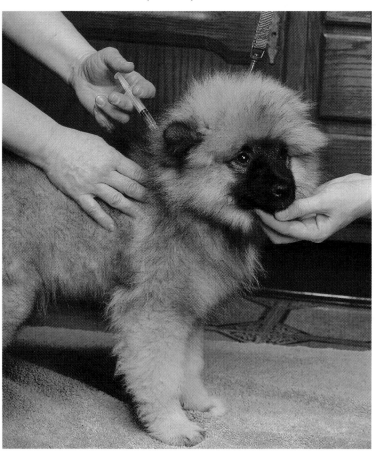

A young puppy is very vulnerable to outside diseases, so take precautions to keep him protected and healthy.

puppy, presumably the breeder has seen to the vaccinations up to the time you acquired custody. Veterinarians differ in their vaccination protocol. It is not unusual for your puppy to have received vaccinations for distemper, hepatitis, leptospirosis, parvovirus and parainfluenza every two to three weeks from the age of five or six weeks. Usually this is a combined injection and is typically called the DHLPP. The DHLPP is given through at least 12 to 14 weeks of age, and it is customary to continue with another parvovirus vaccine at 16 to 18 weeks. You may wonder why so many immunizations are necessary. No one knows for sure when the puppy's maternal antibodies are gone, although it is customarily accepted that distemper antibodies are gone by 12 weeks. Usually parvovirus antibodies are gone by 16 to 18 weeks of age. However, it is possible for the maternal antibodies to be gone at a much earlier age or even a later age. Therefore immunizations are started at an early age. The

vaccine will not give immunity as long as there are maternal antibodies.

The rabies vaccination is given at three or six months of age depending on your local laws. A vaccine for bordetella (kennel cough) is advisable and can be given anytime from the age of five weeks. The coronavirus is not commonly given unless there is a problem locally. The Lyme vaccine is necessary in endemic areas. Lyme disease has been reported in 47 states.

Distemper

This is virtually an incurable disease. If the dog recovers, he is subject to severe nervous disorders. The virus attacks every tissue in the body and resembles a bad cold with a fever. It can cause a runny nose and eyes and cause gastrointestinal disorders, including a poor appetite, vomiting and diarrhea. The virus is carried by raccoons, foxes, wolves, mink and other dogs. Unvaccinated youngsters and senior citizens are very susceptible. This is still a common disease.

Hepatitis

This is a virus that is most serious in very young dogs. It is spread by contact with an infected animal or its stool or urine. The virus affects the liver and kidneys and is characterized by high fever, depression and lack of appetite. Recovered animals may be afflicted with chronic illnesses.

Leptospirosis

This is a bacterial disease transmitted by contact with the urine of an infected dog, rat or other wildlife. It produces severe symptoms of fever, depression, jaundice and internal bleeding and was fatal before the vaccine was developed. Recovered dogs can be carriers, and the disease can be transmitted from dogs to humans.

Maintaining your Keeshond puppy's immunization schedule and booster shots will help him live a long and healthy life.

Parvovirus

This was first noted in the late 1970s and is still a fatal disease. However, with proper vaccinations, early diagnosis and prompt treatment, it is a manageable disease. It attacks the bone marrow and intestinal tract. The symptoms include depression, loss of appetite, vomiting, diarrhea and collapse. Immediate medical attention is of the essence.

Rabies

This is shed in the saliva and is carried by raccoons, skunks, foxes, other dogs and cats. It attacks nerve tissue, resulting in paralysis and death. Rabies can be transmitted to people and is virtually always fatal. This disease is reappearing in the suburbs.

Bordetella (Kennel Cough)

The symptoms are coughing, sneezing, hacking and retching accompanied by nasal discharge usually lasting from a few days to several weeks. There are several disease-producing organisms responsible for this disease. The present vaccines are helpful but do not protect for all the strains. It usually is not life threatening but in some instances it can progress to a serious bronchopneumonia. The disease is highly contagious. The vaccination should be given routinely for dogs that come in contact with other dogs, such as through boarding, training class or visits to the groomer.

Coronavirus

This is usually self limiting and not life threatening. It was first noted in the late '70s about a year before parvovirus. The virus produces a yellow/brown stool and there may be depression, vomiting and diarrhea.

Lyme Disease

This was first diagnosed in the United States in 1976 in Lyme, CT, in people who lived in close proximity to the deer tick. Symptoms may include acute lameness, fever, swelling of joints and loss of appetite. Your veterinarian can advise you if you live in an endemic area.

After your puppy has completed his puppy vaccinations, you will continue to booster the DHLPP once a year. It is customary to booster the rabies one year after the first vaccine and then, depending on where you live, it should be boostered every year or every three years. This depends on your local laws. The Lyme and corona vaccines are boostered annually and it is recommended that the bordetella be boostered every six to eight months.

ANNUAL VISIT

I would like to impress the importance of the annual check up, which would include the booster vaccinations, check for intestinal parasites and test for heartworm. Today in our very busy world it is rush, rush and see "how much you can get for how little." Unbelievably, some non-veterinary businesses have entered into the vaccination business. More harm than good can come to your dog through improper vaccinations, possibly from inferior vaccines and/or the wrong schedule. More than likely you truly care about your companion dog and over the years you have devoted much time and expense to his well being. Perhaps you are unaware that a vaccination is not just a vaccination. There is more involved. Please, please follow

Bordetella attached to canine cilia. Otherwise known as kennel cough, this highly contagious disease should be vaccinated against.

through with regular physical examinations. It is so important for your veterinarian to know your dog and this is especially true during middle age through the geriatric years. More than likely your older dog will require more than one physical a year. The annual physical is good preventive medicine. Through early diagnosis and subsequent treatment your dog can maintain a longer and better quality of life.

INTESTINAL PARASITES

Hookworms

These are almost microscopic intestinal worms that can

cause anemia and therefore serious problems, including death, in young puppies. Hookworms can be transmitted to humans through penetration of the skin. Puppies may be born with them.

Roundworms

These are spaghetti-like worms that can cause a potbellied appearance and dull coat along with more severe symptoms, such as vomiting, diarrhea and coughing. Puppies acquire these while in the mother's uterus and through lactation. Both hookworms and roundworms may be acquired through ingestion.

Whipworms

These have a three-month life cycle and are not acquired through the dam. They cause intermittent diarrhea usually with mucus. Whipworms are possibly the most difficult worm to eradicate. Their eggs are very resistant to most environmental factors and can last for years until the proper conditions enable them to mature. Whipworms are seldom seen in the stool.

Hookworms are almost microscopic intestinal worms that can cause anemia and therefore serious problems, even death.

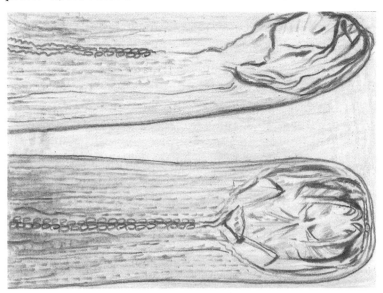

Intestinal parasites are more prevalent in some areas than others. Climate, soil and contamination are big factors contributing to the incidence of intestinal parasites. Eggs are passed in the stool, lay on the ground and then become infective in a certain number of days. Each of the above worms has a different life cycle. Your best chance of becoming and remaining worm-free is to always pooper-scoop your yard. A fenced-in yard keeps stray dogs out, which is certainly helpful.

I would recommend having a fecal examination on your dog twice a year or more often if there is a problem. If your dog has a positive fecal sample, then he will be given the appropriate medication and you will be asked to bring back another stool sample in a certain period of time (depending on the type of worm) and then be rewormed. This process goes on until he has at least two negative samples. The different types of worms require different medications. You will be wasting your money and doing your dog an injustice by buying over-the-counter medication without first consulting your veterinarian.

OTHER INTERNAL PARASITES

Coccidiosis and Giardiasis

These protozoal infections usually affect puppies, especially in places where large numbers of puppies are brought together. Older dogs may harbor these infections but do not show signs unless they are stressed. Symptoms include diarrhea, weight loss and lack of appetite. These infections are not always apparent in the fecal examination.

Roundworm eggs, as would be seen on a fecal evaluation. The eggs must develop for at least 12 days before they are infective.

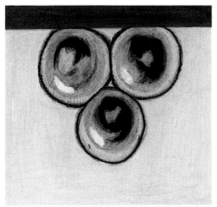

Tapeworms

Seldom apparent on fecal floatation, they are diagnosed frequently as rice-like segments around

the dog's anus and the base of the tail. Tapeworms are long, flat and ribbon like, sometimes several feet in length, and made up of many segments about five-eighths of an inch long. The two most common types of tapeworms found in the dog are:

(1) First the larval form of the flea tapeworm parasite must mature in an intermediate host, the flea, before it can become infective. Your dog acquires this by ingesting the flea through licking and chewing.

(2) Rabbits, rodents and certain large game animals serve as intermediate hosts for other species of tapeworms. If your dog should eat one of these infected hosts, then he can acquire tapeworms.

HEARTWORM DISEASE

This is a worm that resides in the heart and adjacent blood vessels of the lung that produces microfilaria, which circulate in the bloodstream. It is possible for a dog to be infected with any number of worms from one to a hundred that can be 6 to 14 inches long. It is a life-threatening disease, expensive to treat and easily prevented. Depending on where you live, your veterinarian may recommend a preventive year-round and either an annual or semiannual blood test. The most common preventive is given once a month.

EXTERNAL PARASITES

Fleas

These pests are not only the dog's worst enemy but also enemy to the owner's pocketbook. Preventing is less expensive than treating, but regardless we'd prefer to spend our money elsewhere. Likely, the majority of our dogs are allergic to the bite of a flea, and in many cases it only takes one flea bite. The protein in the flea's saliva is the culprit. Allergic dogs have a reaction, which usually results in a "hot spot." More than likely such a reaction will involve a trip to the veterinarian for treatment. Yes, prevention is less expensive. Fortunately today there are several good products available.

Check your Keeshond's coat for parasites like fleas and ticks after he has been playing outside.

If there is a flea infestation, no one product is going to correct the problem. Not only will the dog require treatment so will the environment. In general flea collars are not very effective although there is now available an "egg" collar that will kill the eggs on the dog. Dips are the most economical but they are messy. There are some effective shampoos and treatments available through pet shops and veterinarians. An oral tablet arrived on the American market in 1995 and was popular in Europe the previous year. It sterilizes the female flea but will not kill adult fleas. Therefore the tablet, which is given monthly, will decrease the flea population but is not a "cure-all." Those dogs that suffer from flea-bite allergy will still be subjected to the bite of the flea. Another popular parasiticide is permethrin, which is applied to the back of the dog in one or two places depending on the dog's weight. This product works as a repellent causing the flea to get "hot feet" and jump off. Do not confuse this product with some of the organophosphates that are also applied to the dog's back.

Some products are not usable on young puppies. Treating fleas should be done under your veterinarian's guidance. Frequently it is necessary to combine products and the layman does not have the knowledge regarding possible toxicities. It is hard to believe but there are a few dogs that do have a natural resistance to fleas. Nevertheless it would be wise to treat all pets at the same time. Don't forget your cats. Cats just love to prowl the neighborhood and consequently return with unwanted guests.

Adult fleas live on the dog but their eggs drop off the dog into the environment. There they go through four larval stages before reaching adulthood, and thereby are able to jump back on the poor unsuspecting dog. The cycle resumes and takes between 21 to 28 days under ideal conditions. There are environmental products available that will kill both the adult fleas and the larvae.

Ticks

Ticks carry Rocky Mountain Spotted Fever, Lyme disease and can cause tick paralysis. They should be removed with tweezers, trying to pull out the head. The jaws carry disease. There is a tick preventive collar that does an excellent job. The ticks automatically back out on those dogs wearing collars.

Sarcoptic Mange

This is a mite that is difficult to find on skin scrapings. The pinnal reflex is a good indicator of this disease. Rub the ends of the pinna (ear) together and the dog will start scratching with his foot. Sarcoptes are highly contagious to other dogs and to humans although they do not live long on humans. They cause intense itching.

Demodectic Mange

This is a mite that is passed from the dam to her puppies. It affects youngsters age three to ten months. Diagnosis is confirmed by skin scraping. Small areas of alopecia around the eyes, lips and/or forelegs become visible. There is little itching unless there is a secondary bacterial infection. Some breeds are afflicted more than others.

If you are concerned about your Keeshond contracting ticks, always check his coat thoroughly after playing outdoors.

Cheyletiella

This causes intense itching and is diagnosed by skin scraping. It lives in the outer layers of the skin of dogs, cats, rabbits and humans. Yellow-gray scales may be found on the back and the rump, top of the head and the nose.

TO BREED OR NOT TO BREED

More than likely your breeder has requested that you have your puppy neutered or spayed. Your breeder's request is based on what is healthiest for your dog and what is most beneficial for your breed. Experienced and conscientious breeders devote many years into developing a bloodline. In order to do this, he makes every effort to plan each breeding in regard to conformation, temperament and health. This type of breeder does his best to perform the necessary testing (i.e., OFA, CERF, testing for inherited blood disorders, thyroid, etc.). Testing is expensive and sometimes very disheartening when a favorite dog doesn't pass his health tests. The health history pertains not only to the breeding stock but to the immediate ancestors. Reputable breeders do not want their offspring to be bred indiscriminately. Therefore you may be asked to neuter or spay your puppy. Of course there is always the

Most breeders will ask that you have your pet spayed or neutered. Breeding requires a great amount of knowledge about the breed and should not be taken lightly.

Spaying or neutering your dog can increase his or her chances of living a longer and healthier life.

exception, and your breeder may agree to let you breed your dog under his direct supervision. This is an important concept. More and more effort is being made to breed healthier dogs.

Spay/Neuter

There are numerous benefits of performing this surgery at six months of age. Unspayed females are subject to mammary and ovarian cancer. In order to prevent mammary cancer she must be spayed prior to her first heat cycle. Later in life, an unspayed female may develop a pyometra (an infected uterus), which is definitely life threatening.

Spaying is performed under a general anesthetic and is easy on the young dog. As you might expect it is a little harder on the older dog, but that is no reason to deny her the surgery. The surgery removes the ovaries and uterus. It is important to remove all the ovarian tissue. If some is left behind, she could remain attractive to males. In order to view the ovaries, a reasonably long incision is necessary. An ovariohysterectomy is considered major surgery.

Neutering the male at a young age will inhibit some characteristic male behavior that owners frown upon. Some boys will not hike their legs and mark territory if they are neutered at six months of age. Also neutering at a young age has hormonal benefits, lessening the chance of hormonal aggressiveness.

Breeding only the best-quality dogs ensures that the Keeshond will stay free of hereditary diseases.

Surgery involves removing the testicles but leaving the scrotum. If there should be a retained testicle, then he definitely needs to be neutered before the age of two or three years. Retained testicles can develop into cancer. Unneutered males are at risk for testicular cancer, perineal fistulas, perianal tumors and fistulas and prostatic disease.

Intact males and females are prone to housebreaking accidents. Females urinate frequently before, during and after heat cycles, and males tend to mark territory if there is a female in heat. Males may show the same behavior if there is a visiting dog or guests.

Surgery involves a sterile operating procedure equivalent to human surgery. The incision site is shaved, surgically scrubbed and draped. The veterinarian wears a sterile surgical gown, cap, mask and gloves. Anesthesia should be monitored by a registered technician. It is customary for the veterinarian to recommend a pre-anesthetic blood screening, looking for metabolic problems and a ECG rhythm strip to check for normal heart function. Today anesthetics are equal to human anesthetics, which enables your dog to walk out of the clinic the same day as surgery.

Some folks worry about their dog gaining weight after being neutered or spayed. This is usually not the case. It is true that some dogs may be less active so they could develop a problem, but most dogs are just as active as they were before surgery. However, if your dog should begin to gain, then you need to decrease his food and see to it that he gets a little more exercise.

DENTAL CARE for Your Dog's Life

So you've got a new puppy! You also have a new set of puppy teeth in your household. Anyone who has ever raised a puppy is abundantly aware of these new teeth. Your puppy will chew anything he can reach, chase your shoelaces, and play "tear the rag" with any piece of clothing it can find. When puppies are newly born, they have no teeth. At about four weeks of age, puppies of most breeds begin to develop their deciduous or baby teeth. They begin eating semi-solid food, fighting and biting with their litter mates, and learning discipline from their mother. As their new teeth come in, they inflict more pain on their mother's breasts, so her feeding sessions become less frequent and shorter. By six or eight weeks, the mother will start growling to warn her pups when they are fighting too roughly or hurting her as they nurse too much with their new teeth.

Puppies need to chew. It is a necessary part of their physical and mental development. They develop muscles and necessary life skills as they drag objects around, fight over possession, and vocalize alerts and warnings. Puppies chew on things to explore their world. They are using their sense of taste to determine what is food and what is not. How else can they tell an electrical cord from a lizard? At about four months of age, most puppies begin shedding their baby teeth. Often these teeth need some help to come out and make way for the permanent teeth. The incisors (front teeth) will be replaced first. Then, the adult canine or fang teeth erupt. When the baby tooth is not shed before the permanent tooth comes in, veterinarians call it a retained deciduous tooth. This condition will often cause gum infections by trapping hair and debris between the permanent tooth and the retained baby tooth. Nylafloss® is an excellent device for puppies to use. They can toss it, drag it, and chew on the many surfaces it presents. The baby teeth can catch in the nylon material, aiding in their removal. Puppies that have adequate chew toys will have less destructive behavior, develop more physically, and have less chance of retained deciduous teeth.

During the first year, your dog should be seen by your veterinarian at regular intervals. Your veterinarian will let you know when to bring in your puppy for vaccinations and parasite examinations. At each visit, your veterinarian should inspect the lips, teeth, and mouth as part of a complete physical examination. You should take some part in the maintenance of your dog's oral health. You should examine your dog's mouth weekly throughout his first year to make sure there are no sores, foreign objects, tooth problems, etc. If your dog drools excessively, shakes its head, or has bad breath, consult your veterinarian. By the time your dog is six months old, the permanent teeth are all in and plaque can start to accumulate on the tooth surfaces. This is when your dog needs to develop good dental-care habits to prevent calculus build-up on its teeth. Brushing is best. That is a fact that cannot be denied. However, some dogs do not like their teeth brushed regularly, or you may not be able to accomplish the task. In

A complete oral exam includes checking your dog's lips, teeth, and mouth.

that case, you should consider a product that will help prevent plaque and calculus build-up.

The Plaque Attackers® and Galileo Bone® are other excellent choices for the first three years of a dog's life. Their shapes

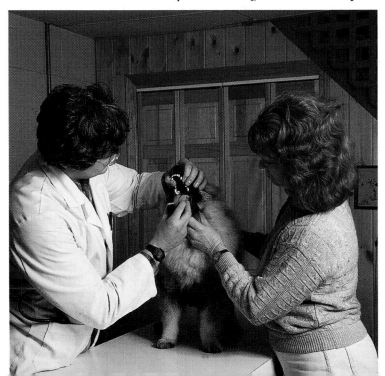

make them interesting for the dog. As the dog chews on them, the solid polyurethane massages the gums which improves the blood circulation to the periodontal tissues. Projections on the chew devices increase the surface and are in contact with the tooth for more efficient cleaning. The unique shape and consistency prevent your dog from exerting excessive force on his own teeth or from breaking off pieces of the bone. If your dog is an aggressive chewer or weighs more than 55 pounds (25 kg), you should consider giving him a Nylabone®, the most durable chew product on the market.

The appropriate toys and bones are excellent tools to relieve your Keeshond's need to chew and keep his teeth and jaw occupied.

The Gumabones ®, made by the Nylabone Company, is constructed of strong polyurethane, which is softer than nylon. Less powerful chewers prefer the Gumabones® to the Nylabones®. A super option for your dog is the Hercules Bone®, a uniquely shaped bone named after the great Olympian for its exception strength. Like all Nylabone products, they are specially scented to make them attractive to your dog. Ask your veterinarian about these bones and he will validate the good doctor's prescription: Nylabones® not only give your dog a good chewing workout but also help to save your dog's teeth (and even his life, as it protects him from possible fatal periodontal diseases).

By the time dogs are four years old, 75 percent of them have periodontal disease. It is the most common infection in dogs. Yearly examinations by your veterinarian are essential to maintaining your dog's good health. If your veterinarian detects periodontal disease, he or she may recommend a prophylactic cleaning. To do a thorough cleaning, it will be necessary to put your dog under anesthesia. With modern gas anesthetics and monitoring equipment, the procedure is pretty safe. Your veterinarian will scale the teeth with an ultrasound scaler or hand instrument. This removes the calculus from the teeth. If there are calculus deposits below the gum line, the veterinarian will plane the roots to make them smooth. After all of the calculus has been removed, the teeth are polished with pumice in a polishing cup. If any medical or surgical treatment is needed, it is done at this time. The final step would be fluoride treatment and your follow-up treatment at

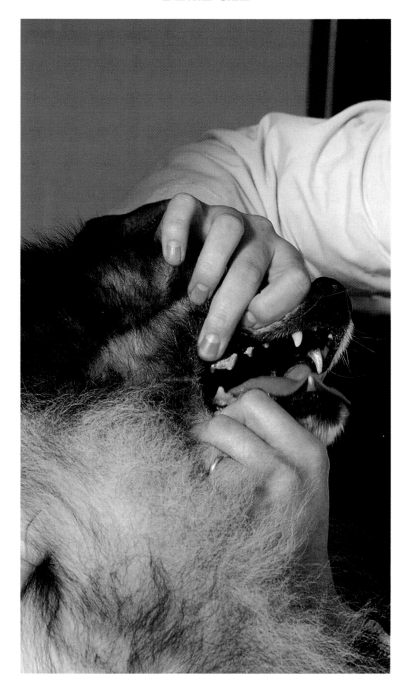

home. If the periodontal disease is advanced, the veterinarian may prescribe a medicated mouth rinse or antibiotics for use at home. Make sure your dog has safe, clean and attractive chew toys and treats. Chooz® treats are another way of using a consumable treat to help keep your dog's teeth clean.

Rawhide is the most popular of all materials for a dog to chew. This has never been good news to dog owners, because rawhide is inherently very dangerous for dogs. Thousands of dogs have died from rawhide, having swallowed the hide after it has become soft and mushy, only to cause stomach and intestinal blockage. A new rawhide product on the market has finally solved the problem of rawhide: molded Roar-Hide® from Nylabone. These are composed of processed, cut up, and melted American rawhide injected into your dog's favorite shape: a dog bone. These dog-safe devices smell and taste like rawhide but don't break up. The ridges on the bones help to fight tartar build-up on the teeth and they last ten times longer than the usual rawhide chews.

As your dog ages, professional examination and cleaning should become more frequent. The mouth should be inspected at least once a year. Your veterinarian may recommend visits every six months. In the geriatric patient, organs such as the heart, liver, and kidneys do not function as well as when they were young. Your veterinarian will probably want to test these organs' functions prior to using general anesthesia for dental cleaning. If your dog is a good chewer and you work closely with your veterinarian, your dog can keep all of its teeth all of its life. However, as your dog ages, his sense of smell, sight, and taste will diminish. He may not have the desire to chase, trap or chew his toys. He will also not have the energy to chew for long periods, as arthritis and periodontal disease make chewing painful. This will leave you with more responsibility for keeping his teeth clean and healthy. The dog that would not let you brush his teeth at one year of age, may let you brush his teeth now that he is ten years old.

Your dog's oral care is just as important as his grooming or nutritional needs. Have his teeth checked at least once a year by your veterinarian.

If you train your dog with good chewing habits as a puppy, he will have healthier teeth throughout his life.

TRAVELING with Your Dog

The earlier you start traveling with your new puppy or dog, the better. He needs to become accustomed to traveling. However, some dogs are nervous riders and become carsick easily. It is helpful if he starts with an empty stomach. Do not despair, as it will go better if you continue taking him with you on short fun rides. How would you feel if every time you rode in the car you stopped at the doctor's for an injection? You would soon dread that nasty car. Older dogs that tend to get carsick may have more of a problem adjusting to traveling. Those dogs that are having a serious problem may benefit from some medication prescribed by the veterinarian.

Do give your dog a chance to relieve himself before getting into the car. It is a good idea to be prepared

A crate is the safest and most effective tool for keeping your dog contained when traveling.

Keep your Keeshond occupied with various chew toys when riding in the car. This way, he will be less likely to distract you while you are driving.

for a clean up with a leash, paper towels, bag and terry cloth towel.

The safest place for your dog is in a fiberglass crate, although close confinement can promote carsickness in some dogs. If your dog is nervous you can try letting him ride on the seat next to you or in someone's lap.

An alternative to the crate would be to use a car harness made for dogs and/or a safety strap attached to the harness or collar. Whatever you do, do not let your dog ride in the back of a pickup truck. I've seen trucks stop quickly and, even though the dog was tied, it fell out and was dragged.

Another advantage of the crate is that it is a safe place to leave him if you need to run into the store. Otherwise you wouldn't be able to leave the windows down. Keep in mind that while many dogs are overly protective in their crates, this may not be enough to deter dognappers. In some states it is against the law to leave a dog in the car unattended.

Never leave a dog loose in the car wearing a collar and leash. More than one dog has killed himself by hanging. Do not let him put his head out an open window. Foreign debris can be blown into his eyes. When leaving your dog unattended in a car, consider the temperature. It can take less than five minutes to reach temperatures over 100 degrees Fahrenheit.

TRIPS

Perhaps you are taking a trip. Give consideration to what is best for your dog—traveling with you or boarding. When traveling by car, van or motor home, you need to think ahead about locking your vehicle. In all probability you have many valuables in the car and do not wish to leave it unlocked. Perhaps most valuable and not replaceable is your dog. Give thought to securing your vehicle and providing adequate ventilation for him. Another consideration for you when traveling with your dog is medical problems that may arise and little inconveniences, such as exposure to external parasites. Some areas of the country are quite flea infested. You may want to carry flea spray with you. This is even a good idea when staying in motels. Quite possibly you are not the only occupant of the room.

Unbelievably many motels and even hotels do allow canine guests, even some very first-class ones. Gaines Pet Foods Corporation publishes *Touring With Towser*, a directory of domestic hotels and motels that accommodate guests with dogs. Their address is Gaines TWT, PO Box 5700, Kankakee, IL, 60902. Call ahead to any motel that you may be considering and see if they accept pets. Sometimes it is necessary to pay a deposit against room damage. The management may feel reassured if you mention that your dog will be crated. If you do travel with your dog, take along plenty of baggies so that you can clean up after him. When we all do our share in cleaning up, we make it possible for motels to continue accepting our pets. As a matter of fact, you should practice cleaning up everywhere you take your dog.

If you have to leave your dog alone inside a vehicle, make sure that it is locked and has plenty of ventilation. Never leave him in the car on a warm day.

Depending on where your are traveling, you may need an up-to-date health certificate issued by

141

your veterinarian. It is good policy to take along your dog's medical information, which would include the name, address and phone number of your veterinarian, vaccination record, rabies certificate, and any medication he is taking.

AIR TRAVEL

When traveling by air, you need to contact the airlines to check their policy. Usually you have to make arrangements up to a couple of weeks in advance for traveling with your dog. The airlines require your dog to travel in an airline approved fiberglass crate. Usually these can be purchased through the airlines but they are also readily available in most pet-supply stores. If your dog is not accustomed to a crate, then it is a good idea to get him acclimated to it before your trip. The day of the actual trip you should withhold water about one hour ahead of departure and no food for about 12 hours. The airlines generally have

It's a good idea to take along your dog's medical records when traveling, which include the name, address, and phone number of your vet, vaccination record, rabies certificate, and any medication he is taking.

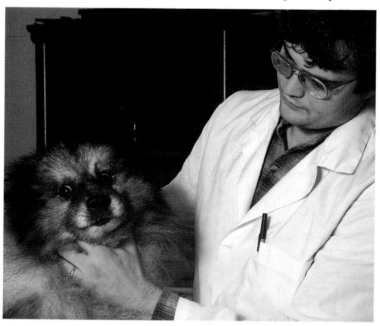

temperature restrictions, which do not allow pets to travel if it is either too cold or too hot. Frequently these restrictions are based on the temperatures at the departure and arrival airports. It's best to inquire about a health certificate. These usually need to be issued within ten days of departure. You should arrange for non-stop, direct flights and if a commuter plane should be involved, check to see if it will carry dogs. Some don't. The Humane Society of the United States has put together a tip sheet for airline traveling. You can receive a copy by sending a self-addressed stamped envelope to:

Keeshonden are a very agreeable and accommodating breed that you can take almost anywhere.

The Humane Society of the United States
  Tip Sheet
  2100 L Street NW
  Washington, DC 20037.
  Regulations differ for traveling outside of the country and are sometimes changed without notice. Well in advance you need to write or call the appropriate consulate or agricultural department for instructions. Some countries have lengthy quarantines (six months), and countries differ in their rabies vaccination requirements. For instance, it may have to be given at least 30 days ahead of your departure.

Do make sure your dog is wearing proper identification including your name, phone number and city. You never know when you might be in an accident and separated from your dog. Or your dog could be frightened and somehow manage to escape and run away.

Another suggestion would be to carry in-case-of-emergency instructions. These would include the address and phone number of a relative or friend, your veterinarian's name, address and phone number, and your dog's medical information.

BOARDING KENNELS

Perhaps you have decided that you need to board your dog. Your veterinarian can recommend a good boarding facility or possibly a pet sitter that will come to your house. It is customary for the boarding kennel to ask for proof of vaccination for the DHLPP, rabies and bordetella vaccine. The bordetella should have been given within six months of boarding. This is for your protection. If they do not ask for this proof I would not board at their kennel. Ask about flea control. Those dogs that suffer flea-bite allergy can get

If you don't want to leave your Keeshond in a boarding kennel while you travel, perhaps your vet could recommend a responsible and reliable pet sitter.

As long as your Keeshond is well behaved and sociable, he should have no problem staying in a kennel or with a friendly, dog-loving pet sitter.

in trouble at a boarding kennel. Unfortunately boarding kennels are limited on how much they are able to do.

For more information on pet sitting, contact NAPPS:

National Association of Professional Pet Sitters
1200 G Street, NW
Suite 760
Washington, DC 20005.

Some pet clinics have technicians that pet sit and technicians that board clinic patients in their homes. This may be an alternative for you. Ask your veterinarian if they have an employee that can help you. There is a definite advantage of having a technician care for your dog, especially if your dog is on medication or is a senior citizen.

You can write for a copy of *Traveling With Your Pet* from ASPCA, Education Department, 441 E. 92nd Street, New York, NY 10128.

IDENTIFICATION and Finding the Lost Dog

There are several ways of identifying your dog. The old standby is a collar with dog license, rabies, and ID tags. Unfortunately collars have a way of being separated from the dog and tags fall off. We're not suggesting you shouldn't use a collar and tags. If they stay intact and on the dog, they are the quickest way of identification.

For several years owners have been tattooing their dogs. Some tattoos use a number with a registry. Here lies the problem because there are several registries to check. If you wish to tattoo, use your social security number. The humane shelters have the means to trace it. It is usually done on the inside of the rear thigh. The area is first shaved and numbed. There is no pain, although a few dogs do not like the buzzing sound. Occasionally tattooing is not legible and needs to be redone.

The newest method of identification is microchipping. The microchip is a computer chip that is no larger than a grain of rice. The veterinarian implants it by injection between the shoulder blades. The dog feels no discomfort. If your dog is lost and picked up by the humane society, they can trace you by scanning the microchip, which has its own code. Microchip scanners are friendly to other brands of microchips and their registries. The microchip comes with a dog tag saying the dog is microchipped. It is the safest way of identifying your dog.

FINDING THE LOST DOG

I am sure you will agree that there would be little worse than losing your dog. Responsible pet owners rarely lose their dogs. They do not let their dogs run free because they don't want harm to come to them. Not only that but in most, if not all, states there is a leash law.

Beware of fenced-in yards. They can be a hazard. Dogs find ways to escape either over or under the fence. Another fast exit is through the gate that perhaps the neighbor's child left unlocked.

Below is a list that hopefully will be of help to you if you need it. Remember don't give up, keep looking. Your dog is worth your efforts.

1. Contact your neighbors and put flyers with a photo on it in their mailboxes. Information you should include would be the dog's name, breed, sex, color, age, source of identification, when your dog was last seen and where, and your name and phone numbers. It may be helpful to say the dog needs medical care. Offer a *reward*.

2. Check all local shelters daily. It is also possible for your dog to be picked up away from home and end up in an out-of-the-way shelter. Check these too. Go in person. It is not good enough to call. Most shelters are limited on the time they can hold dogs then they are put up for adoption or euthanized. There is the possibility that your dog will not make it to the shelter for several days. Your dog could have been wandering or someone may have tried to keep him.

The newest method of identification is the microchip, a computer chip no bigger than a grain of rice that can help you track your dog's whereabouts.

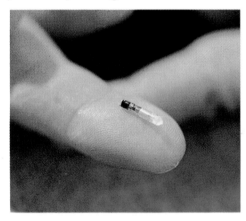

3. Notify all local veterinarians. Call and send flyers.

4. Call your breeder. Frequently breeders are contacted when one of their breed is found.

5. Contact the rescue group for your breed.

6. Contact local schools—children may have seen your dog.

7. Post flyers at the schools, groceries, gas stations, convenience stores, veterinary clinics, groomers and any other place that will allow them.

8. Advertise in the newspaper.

9. Advertise on the radio.

BEHAVIOR and Canine Communication

Studies of the human/animal bond point out the importance of the unique relationships that exist between people and their pets. Those of us who share our lives with pets understand the special part they play through companionship, service, and protection. For many, the pet/owner bond goes beyond simple companionship; pets are often considered members of the family. A leading pet food manufacturer recently conducted a nationwide survey of pet owners to gauge just how important pets were in their lives. Here's what they found:

- 76 percent allow their pets to sleep on their beds
- 78 percent think of their pets as their children
- 84 percent display photos of their pets, mostly in their homes
- 84 percent think that their pets react to their own emotions
- 100 percent talk to their pets
- 97 percent think that their pets understand what they're saying

Are you surprised?

Senior citizens show more concern for their own eating habits when they have the responsibility of feeding a dog. Seeing that their dog is routinely exercised encourages the owner to think of schedules that otherwise may seem unimportant to the senior citizen. The older owner may be arthritic and feeling poorly but with responsibility for his dog he has a reason to get up and get moving. It is a big plus if his dog is an attention seeker who will demand such from his owner.

Over the last couple of decades, it has been shown that pets relieve the stress of those who lead busy lives. Owning a pet has been known to lessen the occurrence of heart attack and stroke.

Many single folks thrive on the companionship of a dog. Lifestyles are very different from a long time ago, and today more individuals seek the single life. However, they receive fulfillment from owning a dog.

Most likely the majority of our dogs live in family environments. The companionship they provide is well worth the effort involved. In my opinion, every child should have the opportunity to have a family dog. Dogs teach responsibility through understanding their care, feelings, and even respecting their life cycles. Frequently those children who have not been exposed to dogs grow up afraid of dogs, which isn't good. Dogs sense timidity and some will take advantage of the situation.

Today more dogs are serving as service dogs. Since the origination of Seeing Eye dogs years ago, we now have trained hearing dogs. Also, dogs are trained to provide service for the handicapped and are able to perform many different tasks for their owners. Search and Rescue dogs, with their handlers, are sent throughout the world to assist in the recovery of disaster victims. They are lifesavers.

Therapy dogs are very popular with nursing homes, and some hospitals even allow them to visit. The inhabitants truly look forward to their visits. They wanted and were allowed to have visiting dogs in their beds to hold and love.

Dogs play a very important role in our lives. It's been proven that pets relieve stress, as well as lessen the occurrence of illness in their owners.

Nationally there is a Pet Awareness Week to educate students and others about the value

149

and basic care of our pets. Many countries take an even greater interest in their pets than Americans do. In those countries the pets are allowed to accompany their owners into restaurants and shops, etc. In the US this freedom is only available to our service dogs. Even so, we think very highly of the human/animal bond.

Canine Behavior

Canine behavior problems are the number-one reason for pet owners to dispose of their dogs, either through new homes, humane shelters, or euthanasia. Unfortunately there are too many owners who are unwilling to devote the necessary time to properly train their dogs. On the other hand, there are those who not only are concerned about inherited health problems but are also aware of the dog's mental stability.

You may realize that a breed and its group relatives (i.e., sporting, hounds, etc.) show tendencies toward behavioral characteristics. An experienced breeder can acquaint you with his breed's personality. Unfortunately many breeds are labeled with poor temperaments when actually the breed as a whole is not affected, only a small percentage of individuals within the breed.

Inheritance and environment contribute to the dog's behavior. Some naïve people suggest inbreeding as the cause of bad temperaments. Inbreeding only results in poor behavior if the ancestors carry the trait. If there are excellent temperaments behind the dogs, then inbreeding will promote good temperaments in the offspring. Did you ever consider that inbreeding is what sets the characteristics of a breed? A purebred dog is the end result of inbreeding. This does not spare the mixed-breed dog from the same problems. Mixed-breed dogs frequently are the offspring of purebred dogs.

The bond between humans and animals, especially a lovable breed like the Keeshond, is a strong one. Who could resist a fluffy ball of fur like this?

Not too many decades ago most of our dogs led a different lifestyle than what is prevalent today. Usually mom stayed home so the dog had human companionship and someone to discipline him if needed. Not much was expected from the dog. Today's mom works and everyone's life is at a much faster pace.

Although busy schedules can make it difficult, make sure that your Keeshond has adequate mental and physical stimulation to keep him happy and satisfied.

The dog may have to adjust to being a "weekend" dog. The family is gone all day during the week, and the dog is left to his own devices for entertainment. Some dogs sleep all day waiting for their families to come home and others become wigwam wreckers if given the opportunity. Crates do ensure the safety of the dog and the house. However, he could become a physical and emotional cripple if he doesn't get enough exercise and attention. We still appreciate and want the companionship of our dogs although we expect more from them. In many cases we tend to forget dogs are just that—*dogs* not human beings.

SOCIALIZING AND TRAINING

Many prospective puppy buyers lack experience regarding the proper socialization and training needed to develop the type of pet we all desire. In the first 18 months, training does take some work. It is easier to start proper training before there is a problem that needs to be corrected.

The initial work begins with the breeder. The breeder should start socializing the puppy at five to six weeks of age and cannot let up. Human socializing is critical up through 12 weeks of age and likewise important during the following months. The litter should be left together during the first few weeks but it is necessary to separate the pups by ten weeks of age. Leaving them together after that time will increase competition for litter dominance. If puppies are not socialized with people by 12 weeks of age, they will be timid in later life.

Breeders should begin socializing their puppies at five to six weeks of age. If puppies are not socialized with people by 12 weeks of age, they will be timid later in life.

The eight- to ten-week age period is a fearful time for puppies. They need to be handled very gently around children and adults. There should be no harsh discipline during this time. Starting at 14 weeks of age, the puppy begins the juvenile period, which ends when he reaches sexual maturity

153

around 6 to 14 months of age. During the juvenile period, he needs to be introduced to strangers (adults, children, and other dogs) on the home property. At sexual maturity he will begin to bark at strangers and become more protective. Males start to lift their legs to urinate, but if you desire you can inhibit this behavior by walking your boy on leash away from trees, shrubs, fences, etc.

Perhaps you are thinking about an older puppy. You need to inquire about the puppy's social experience. If he has lived in a kennel, he may have a hard time adjusting to people and environmental stimuli. Assuming he has had a good social upbringing, there are advantages to an older puppy.

Training includes puppy kindergarten and a minimum of one to two basic training classes. During these classes you will learn how to dominate your youngster. This is especially important if you own a large breed of dog. It is somewhat harder, if not nearly impossible, for some owners to be the alpha figure when their dog towers over them. You will be taught how to properly restrain your dog. This concept is important. Again it puts you in the alpha position. All dogs need to be restrained many times during their lives. Believe it or not, some of our worst offenders are the eight-week-old puppies that are brought to our clinic. They need to be gently restrained for a nail trim but the way they carry on you would think we were killing them. In comparison, their vaccination is a "piece of cake." When we ask dogs to do something that is not agreeable to them, then their worst comes out. Life will be easier for your dog if you expose him at a young age to the necessities of life—proper behavior and restraint.

UNDERSTANDING THE DOG'S LANGUAGE

Most authorities agree that the dog is a descendent of the wolf. The dog and wolf have similar traits. For instance both are pack oriented and prefer not to be isolated for long periods of time. Another characteristic is that the dog, like the wolf, looks to the leader—alpha—for direction. Both the wolf and the dog communicate through body language, not only within their pack but with outsiders.

Every pack has an alpha figure. The dog looks to you, or should look to you, to be that leader. If your dog doesn't receive the proper training and guidance, he very well may replace you as alpha. This would be a serious problem and is certainly a disservice to your dog.

Eye contact is one way the Alpha wolf keeps order within his pack. You are alpha so you must establish eye contact with your puppy. Obviously your puppy will have to look at you. Practice eye contact even if you need to hold his head for five to ten seconds at a time. You can give him a treat as a reward. Make sure your eye contact is gentle and not threatening. Later, if he has been naughty, it is permissible to give him a long, penetrating look. There are some older dogs that never learned eye contact as puppies and cannot accept eye contact. You should avoid eye contact with these dogs since they feel threatened and will retaliate as such.

Your Keeshond should look to you as his leader. Establishing gentle eye contact with him will let him know that you are in charge.

BODY LANGUAGE

The play bow, when the forequarters are down and the hindquarters are elevated, is an invitation to play. Puppies play fight, which helps them learn the acceptable limits of biting. This is

Puppies, like this trio of Keeshonden, are easy to love. However, puppies need a great deal of guidance and a firm set of rules in order to grow into healthy, properly socialized adults.

necessary for later in their lives. Nevertheless, an owner may be falsely reassured by the playful nature of his dog's aggression. Playful aggression toward another dog or human may be an indication of serious aggression in the future. Owners should never play fight or play tug-of-war with any dog that is inclined to be dominant.

Signs of submission are:
1. Avoids eye contact.
2. Active submission—the dog crouches down, ears back, and the tail is lowered.
3. Passive submission—the dog rolls on his side with his hindlegs in the air and frequently urinates.

Signs of dominance are:
1. Makes eye contact.
2. Stands with ears up, tail up, and the hair raised on his neck.
3. Shows dominance over another dog by standing at right angles over it.

Dominant dogs tend to behave in characteristic ways such as:

There are many ways to express dominance over a dog, such as standing over him or staring him in the eyes.

1. The dog may be unwilling to move from his place (i.e., reluctant to give up the sofa if the owner wants to sit there).
2. He may not part with toys or objects in his mouth and may show possessiveness with his food bowl.
3. He may not respond quickly to commands.
4. He may be disagreeable to grooming and dislike being petted.

Dogs are popular because of their sociable nature. Those that have contact with humans during the first 12 weeks of life regard them as a member of their own species–their pack. All dogs have the potential for both dominant and submissive behavior. Only through experience and training do they learn to whom it is appropriate to show which behavior. Not all dogs are concerned with dominance but owners need to be aware of that potential. It is wise for the owner to establish his dominance early on.

A human can express dominance or submission toward a dog in the following ways:

1. Meeting the dog's gaze signals dominance. Averting the gaze signals submission. If the dog growls or threatens, averting the gaze is the first avoiding action to take—it may prevent attack. It is important to establish eye contact with the puppy. The older dog that has not been exposed to eye contact may see it as a threat and will not be willing to submit.

2. Being taller than the dog signals dominance; being lower signals submission. This is why, when attempting to make friends with a strange dog or catch the runaway, one should kneel down to his level. Some owners see their dogs become dominant when allowed on the furniture or on the bed. Then he is at the owner's level.

3. An owner can gain dominance by ignoring all the dog's social initiatives. The owner pays attention to the dog only when he obeys a command.

No dog should be allowed to achieve dominant status over any adult or child. Ways of preventing this are as follows:

1. Handle the puppy gently, especially during the three- to four-month period.

2. Let the children and adults handfeed him and teach him to take food without lunging or grabbing.

3. Do not allow him to chase children or joggers.

4. Do not allow him to jump on people or mount their legs. Even females may be inclined to mount. It is not only a male habit.

5. Do not allow him to growl for any reason.

6. Don't participate in wrestling or tug-of-war games.

7. Don't physically punish a puppy for aggressive behavior. Restrain him from repeating the infraction and teach an alternative behavior. Dogs should earn everything they receive from their owners. This would include sitting to receive petting or treats, sitting before going out the door, and sitting to receive the collar and leash. These types of exercises reinforce the owner's dominance.

Young children should never be left alone with a dog. It is important that children learn some basic obedience commands so they have some control over the dog. They will gain the respect of their dog.